THE
NORTH ATLANTIC
CIVILIZATION

MICHAEL KRAUS

Professor of History
The City College of New York

AN ANVIL ORIGINAL

under the general editorship of

LOUIS L. SNYDER

D. VAN NOSTRAND COMPANY, INC.
PRINCETON, NEW JERSEY
TORONTO　　　　　　　　　　　　　　　　　LONDON
NEW YORK

For My Teachers

Nelson P. Mead   J. Salwyn Schapiro

D. VAN NOSTRAND COMPANY, INC.

120 Alexander St., Princeton, New Jersey (*Principal office*)
257 Fourth Avenue, New York 10, New York
25 Hollinger Rd., Toronto 16, Canada
358, Kensington High Street, London, W.14, England

PREFACE

In Europe and America interest in the concept of the Atlantic community has mounted rapidly in recent years. It is my view that the New World was more than merely another area added to the territory covered by Western European civilization. European civilization underwent important transformations overseas, and out of the interaction of the New World and the Old has come the Atlantic Civilization. It embraces a people who, though welcoming diversity, cherish a unity of belief in human dignity and the values of a democratic society. America added substance to the concepts of political and religious freedom, and favored the realization of humanitarian ideals. The theories were usually conceived in Europe; it was America's gift to demonstrate their practicality.

No country, not even a large region seemingly self-sufficient, lives unrelated to the rest of the world in our time. The peoples and countries included in the North Atlantic Civilization are no island set apart from the rest of mankind. All the world has helped its growth and impinges on it daily. But it has had and continues to have a central place in working out solutions to men's problems of food, health, and shelter. It has been the home of the world's great, in letters, arts, and science. Its vitality, impaired by two world wars, is still impressive. The people of the North Atlantic Civilization must preserve that vitality so that men everywhere, invigorated by it, may come to live in freedom.

I wish to express my gratitude to the Guggenheim Foundation for the fellowship that enabled me to gather some of the material in this volume. I should like to acknowledge, too, the helpful suggestions of my colleague Louis L. Snyder.

New York, New York   M. K.
August, 1957

TABLE OF CONTENTS

Part One

THE NORTH ATLANTIC
CIVILIZATION

— 1 —

INTRODUCTION: WHAT IS THE ATLANTIC CIVILIZATION?

Patterns of Civilization. Historians have long accepted well-established eras such as those of the Sumerian civilization, the Egyptian, the Hellenic and Hellenistic, the Roman, and the Moslem civilization, and the medieval civilization of Europe. During the centuries in which each of these civilizations existed and throughout the lands under its sway, historians have discerned common threads which gave a recognizable pattern to that specific civilization. It might be language and art forms (as in Hellenic and Hellenistic civilizations); it might be language, law, and forms of administration (as in Roman civilization); it might be language, art forms (including literature) and religion (as in medieval Europe). Educated Greeks could travel through all the lands living in the light of their civilization and find themselves at home with cultured people in Italy, Egypt, or Asia Minor. They often spoke the same language, quoted the same writers, and had very much the same view of life.

Medieval Civilization. What was possible for cultured Greeks in the scattered lands of the Mediterranean was likewise possible for the succeeding Romans, and impressively so for Christians in Latin Europe of the Middle Ages. The Europe which came under the influence of Latin Christian civilization, though revealing local differences in economy and folk traditions, did have a distinguishing cultural unity. The educated person moving from one region to another in the large geographical area arched over by Latin Christianity did not feel himself altogether an alien in lands foreign to his birthplace.

For many centuries the geographical center of the unified civilized world of the West (there were civilizations, too, in the East) was the Mediterranean. Lines of communication, rivers and roads, linked Europe's interior with this basin. The cross-fertilization of cultures in this fruitful area constantly invigorated European society. Europe's northern lands felt the impact of the civilization of Persia and the Near East by transmission via the rivers of Russia and the Baltic Sea.

The Medieval World Disrupted. The relative unity of the medieval world was succeeded by a disruptive era which accented differences rather than similarities between peoples. The rise of Protestantism, the growth of national states, the imperial rivalries born of overseas discoveries, all played their divisive parts in the European community. It should be remembered, however, that the unity of medieval Europe can be exaggerated in our thinking. Apart from religion, much of what we speak of as that era's unity was apparent only to the educated minority. Rivalries between feudal princes were as divisive as those between kings; wars between city states were as unsettling as those between nations.

Europe and America. Nevertheless it is correct to say that the Europe of the sixteenth century and after was different from what it had once been. Among the factors that newly shaped it was the discovery of America. A vast frontier lavished its plenty on Europe, broadening the Old World's margin of physical subsistence as well as its mental horizon. From the seas that bordered America, from its mines, its fields, its forests came the wealth that gave impetus to Europe's slow-growing capitalism. In turn Europe's labor, increased capital, and inventiveness further exploited New World resources. But Europe gave much more to transatlantic settlers. She endowed them with a rich cultural heritage which, despite some neglect common to pioneers in new lands, was preserved.

English colonists, in particular, made strenuous efforts not only to preserve it but to enhance it. They were especially successful in enlarging the area of political freedom available to the lowly as well as to the high-born. The Americans strove also (following English precedent) to increase cultural opportunities for the unprivileged along with the prosperous. America's example of religious liberty and separation of church and state inspired soul-searching among Europeans, and finally emulation. The accent on human dignity which marked the emergence of the libertarian tradition in seventeenth-century Europe was reenforced in the American environment. Above all, the Anglo-American community was committed to the rule of law which made individuals and institutions subject to it. It was a society inhospitable to absolutism.

Impact of America.   From America, especially after its Revolution and Declaration of Independence, came influences hostile to authoritarianism in politics, religion, and economics. The English revolutions of the seventeenth century had laid the foundations for such hostility. The American and French revolutions in the next century fixed more firmly the objectives of those opposed to traditional authoritarianism. The nineteenth and twentieth centuries have seen the fulfillment of much of the liberal political and social program of earlier years.

The North Atlantic Community.   Out of the play of influences crossing the sea westward and eastward emerged a sense of community sufficiently distinctive to be called the Atlantic Civilization. Though it may be said to embrace the whole Western Hemisphere and much of Europe (and even African Negro culture), the areas most vigorously committed to its ideals are North America and western Europe. While in earlier civilizations only educated people had a common culture that transcended local boundaries, in the Atlantic Civilization the great mass of men as well as the elite have held mutually profitable exchanges. With the development of mass communications the "Americanization" of Europe has been greatly accelerated. The center of power in the Atlantic community has shifted from its original home in western Europe across the sea to America.

In our own time we have become sharply aware of the impact of each area upon the other in the Atlantic community, but the latter's creation has been the product of centuries. Despite the apparent sudden flowering of the Atlantic Civilization it has been of slow growth. What has been created is one of the greatest achievements in man's history.

— 2 —

AN ATLANTIC CIVILIZATION EMERGES

"Since 1917, at latest, the U.S.A. has been as much a European power as England. Only too much like England in being slow to recognize the solidarity of her political interests with those of geographical Europe." Thus mused Bernhard Berenson during World War II. Americans were indeed slow to recognize the intimate relationship of their political interests with those of Europe; but once they were shocked into recognition of that tie, they made a commendable effort to shoulder the burden of leadership in the Atlantic world, as well as in other regions of our shrunken globe. Europe, it would appear, is the greatest fact in North America. And in the consciousness of Europeans it seems that for them the greatest fact is the power and influence of the United States.

Asian Impact on Europe. Europeans, in the centuries before Columbus, had gone to far and strange places where exotic scenes and people had stirred the traveler's imagination. From older civilizations in the East, whence wealth flowed west, the European learned to beautify his home and garden and exercise his mind in studying Oriental philosophy. In the long run, however, it was the impact from the new lands bordering the Atlantic that shook more profoundly the structure of European society. Europe's masses were not much affected by upper-class devotion to Chinese gardens, furniture, or philosophy. What came from the New World, especially that which was distilled from the experiences of fellow countrymen transplanted, was embedded more deeply in the pattern of European life. Into the consciousness of Europeans still at home were absorbed the hopes and frustrations of transatlantic settlers. (*See Reading No. 1.*)

American Impact Greater.   America was a powerful stimulus to Europe's imagination. The literary mind fed on the strange and wondrous regions that lay beyond the familiar seascape. Men of letters in the Elizabethan Age found sustenance in the fertility of travelers' tales. And even in later years these racy narratives continued to invigorate the imagination. Coleridge created the eeriness of the *Rime of the Ancient Mariner* by blending the language of the voyagers into his poetry.

Exotic peoples made Europeans conscious of the limitations of their own civilization because their own failings seemed accentuated when contrasted with the alleged superiority of primitives. The most highly regarded of these primitives were the American Indians, the best known of the "noble savages." Their supposed natural, spontaneous way of life with its stress on liberty and equality was held up as inspiration to tradition-bound Europe, fettered in an aristocratic chain of command. The "noble savage," portrayed in words and pictures of brilliant color, excited Europeans who now found their own civilization drab.

The stimulus from overseas can be traced in many directions. Anthropologists (the word was coined in the seventeenth century) now doubted the descent of all men from one pair. The New World, said one writer, contained such varieties of men and animals unknown to Asia or Africa that their origin was uncertain and surely challenged the theory that all the earth was planted from one little spot. The question was raised, where did the American Indian come from? And it was quickly surmised that he had come from eastern Asia.

The interaction between the peoples of the Old World and the New gradually produced a new civilization. As a writer in the eighteenth century phrased it, the discovery and exploitation of vast western regions extended geographical knowledge, "perfected navigation, opened new sources of commerce, and gave a new face even to the affairs of Europe."

Overseas Economic Influence on Europe.   The everyday life of people was deeply affected by the streams of precious metals that flowed from America into Spain and thence to the rest of Europe, inflating prices and accelerating the rate of change in the local economy. Slowly, wage rates were adjusted to commodity price increases. Europe's economists usually coupled internal situations with transatlantic realities. Englishmen argued that overseas trade would promote home employment and cut down poverty and highway robbery, and colonial settlements would lift paupers from overburdened parishes. Sir Josiah Child, before the end of the seventeenth century, estimated that the plantation colonies, especially the West Indies, were already giving employment to 200,000 people in England. (*See Reading No. 2.*)

The fortunes of France, too, were heavily involved in the West Indies. Her trade with the Antilles in sugar, coffee, indigo, cottonwood, etc. was about one-quarter of her whole volume of foreign commerce on the eve of her Revolution in 1789. In these same years William Pitt believed that England's annual income from West Indian plantations was £4,000,000; it was this accumulation of capital, along with that from India in Asia which helped finance the Industrial Revolution. Adam Smith thought that trade with America was more valuable to Europe than that with the East Indies.

Overseas commodities became available to greater numbers of Europeans in the eighteenth century. Tea and sugar, once luxuries, became more widely familiar. Tobacco, imported and reexported in great quantities (100,-000,000 lb. to Britain in one year, shortly before American Independence) became a powerful force in the Atlantic economy, its transportation and retail distribution furnishing jobs to hundreds of thousands. New foods —maize, the tomato, the potato—won a place in European diets, and for the poor in particular, corn and the potato became staple foods. The Germans and the Irish depending too heavily on the potato were fearfully vulnerable in times of famine, but in the main, potatoes made life secure enough to support a vast increase in population in the eighteenth and nineteenth centuries.

Effect on Europe's Class Structure. This trade which changed the psychology of class relationships made society more fluid. It gave, said Henry Fielding, "a new face to the whole nation, and hath almost totally changed the manners, customs, and habits of the people, more especially of the lower sort"; their humility was changed into pride, "and their subjection into equality." It was particularly in lands across the sea in America that a greater liberation of man's spirit was achieved. (*See Reading No. 3.*)

Communications Between Europe and America. Newspapers and magazines, more frequent travel and better postal facilities made America a topic of everyday conversation. The New World did not seem as remote to Europeans in the eighteenth century as we generally imagine. They took for granted the slowness of communications and adjusted accordingly. Though fast boats often made the transatlantic voyage in four weeks, longer periods were more common.

The ties of communities on the rim of the Atlantic basin were already so close as to make them matters of deep concern to the peoples involved. Crop failures in Europe would draw off so much wheat that embargoes were imposed to prevent hardship in the colonies. On the other hand, quantities of American wheat arriving in European ports forced a lowering of local prices.

Commodities going east and manufactures and emigrants moving west kept a large number of vessels busy. Joining the westbound migrants were Europeans visiting the New World to see its wilderness, to roam over its varied immensity, and to watch the emergence of a new society. Eastbound were American merchants, clergy, officials, and tourists sailing to see the sights in London and Paris which their descendants have never ceased to admire. Along with them went young men to study law in London, medicine in Edinburgh, or to loll in more leisurely fashion over their books at Oxford or Cambridge. The famous British philologist, Sir William Jones, thought his young countrymen should finish their education by visiting the United States "instead of fluttering about Italy"; they should learn political wisdom from American republicans rather than pick up "a few superficial notions of the fine arts" from narrow-minded, superstitious Italians.

Forecasting American Power. During the years of increasing friction between England and her colonies prophetic voices in the homeland recognized that the increase of American population would be a notable addition to British power and wealth. America's weight, it was said, would enable England to maintain the traditional balance of power. Men with limited views, however, could only think of America as an economic competitor whose full strength was soon to be revealed. On the eve of the Revolution they outnumbered the far-seeing ones who, with a vision of Anglo-American destiny, had almost grasped the true nature of an Atlantic commonwealth. (*See Reading No. 4.*)

Religious Ties. The ties that linked inhabitants across the ocean were many. Trade and imperial politics joined (though they sometimes divided) distant lands. Religion too was a bond of union, as well as a spur to dissension. The Anglican Church, secure as the established faith, embraced the colonies in its broad beneficence, winning converts and promoting learning through its missionary agency, the Society for the Promotion of the Gospel (S.P.G.). But it was offensive to many nonconformists in the colonies—Congregationalists, Presbyterians, Baptists, and Quakers.

The nonconforming sects ordinarily supplied the energy for religious change and adjustment. The Dissenters in the eighteenth century, in England and America, were far and away the most political-minded people of their time, often strong advocates of civil and religious liberty.

In the renewal of religious life that men and women experienced in America and Europe in the mid-eighteenth century, Moravians, Wesleyans, Quakers, and others temporarily brushed aside the limiting barriers of sectarianism. John Wesley on his voyage to Georgia in 1735, in company with Moravians, enjoyed a genuine spiritual rebirth. In Georgia he slowly molded the organization of Methodism. The circuit itinerant ministry, the love feast, leaders and lay assistants, extemporaneous preaching and prayer, and much more besides, it is claimed, came to Wesley in America and thence was transplanted to British country towns and cities. On the other hand, German Pietism, the base of its flame in Halle, enkindled England and America.

The American revival mingling with German Pietism and English Methodism added its power to the renewal of religion. It was George Whitefield, a powerful preacher, who more than any other single personality stirred the Anglo-American world in a common emotion. He thought America a spacious land for his boundless energy, and he communicated to others his belief. "Fear not to speak the truth," he wrote to a preacher in Yorkshire; "if driven out of England, here is a noble range for you in America." (*See Reading No. 5.*)

Common Anglo-American Literary Background. Just as common religious experiences united people on both sides of the Atlantic, so did the establishment of schools, the creation of libraries, and the sale of books. Nearly all the colleges in America benefited from British philanthropy, their bookshelves enriched by foreign donations, while forceful personalities such as John Witherspoon, the Scotsman at Princeton, furnished educational leadership to the colonies. (*See Reading No. 6.*)

American and British children often read the same books. Inexpensive works were published in America; but for costly publications or books with a limited audience, American readers ordinarily had to look abroad. The most significant influences in education traveled from east to west; for example, the organization and curriculum of the colleges. In at least one important matter, however —supplying texts for youngsters—Lindley Murray, a transplanted colonial living in Britain after the Revolution, made a valuable contribution to the Atlantic community. His *Grammar,* in particular, said to be the best of its kind, had a wide acceptance in Britain and in his native America.

Franklin thought that English authors were not sufficiently aware of their fame in America. A vast audience was assembling there, he said, for "English Authors, ancient, present and future." His own writings had a large and eager response abroad. Indeed, a London magazine thought Franklin was better known in Europe than in his native country, and it expressed the universal impatience with which his memoirs were awaited. When they finally were given to the world it responded with delight and placed them with the literary classics. The rapid growth of the Atlantic British Empire inspired prophecies that English would some day displace French as the most popular language for international usage.

America and a Democratic Culture. In the colonial era America was heavily dependent upon the homeland for stimulation in literature and education. While original creation was uncommon in the New World the pressure among Americans was always for broadening opportunities so that a larger audience could enjoy the fruits of genius. In England, too, this tendency was apparent though not so marked. Americans spoke proudly of their democratization of educational institutions such as schools and libraries. To enlarge the area of educational opportunity was already their fixed objective.

America and Art. "After the first Cares for the Necessaries of Life are over, we shall come to think of the Embellishments," wrote Franklin to a favorite correspondent. "Already some of our young Geniuses begin to lisp Attempts at Painting, Poetry and Musick." The young men he referred to were hardly geniuses in poetry and music, but were nearer the mark in painting.

John Singleton Copley and Benjamin West were colonial painters who moved across the Atlantic into the larger art world of London to receive the plaudits of the great. West was one of the first, said a London magazine, "who opened the eyes of the English to the merits of modern Historical Painting, and excited in them a desire of seeing it flourish in this happy Island." Copley's contribution to historical painting was possibly of even greater artistic value than that of West. Vast crowds went to see Copley's "The Death of the Earl of Chatham" and "The Defeat of the Floating Batteries at Gibraltar."

Americans, though proud of the acclaim won by expatriates, often regretted the circumstances that forced them to leave their native land. There was doleful agreement with artists' complaints of inadequate patronage and poorly developed taste. The sense of inferiority experienced by colonial Americans when contemplating the superior achievements of European artists, was transmitted to subsequent generations.

It was to be expected that transplanted Europeans should bring with them to the New World their familiar forms of architecture, their church music and folk songs. New settings, however, soon dictated changes in house design. Wealthy Southerners preferred homes of greater airiness than was found in English prototypes. The Swedes, on the Delaware, carried into the American wilderness their log cabin, which proved to be most adaptable to the frontier. By the time of the Revolution this had become the typical dwelling of frontiersmen.

Jefferson and the Arts. Jefferson told Madison he was an enthusiast on the subject of the arts, and his object was to improve the taste of his countrymen. He was insistent that public buildings be a standing guide to architectural excellence.

Jefferson was part of a small American circle whose tastes were of a standard comparable to the best European level. But the mass of Americans, like people elsewhere, had limited esthetic experience; and even where a sense of beauty was well developed, there were not always the means to indulge it. Franklin bemoaned the fact that the best American artists went to Europe where people were rich enough to employ them. The lamentations of the artist in unappreciative America, which sounded so loud and insistent in the nineteenth and twentieth centuries, were but the magnified echo of complaints in colonial times.

Humanitarianism. Although Americans apologized, to excess, for their limitations in the fine arts, they showed greater confidence in dealing with problems of human relationships. Just as on religious questions they felt they had much to teach Europe, so, too, in proposals to temper man's inhumanity to man colonials expressed themselves with assurance. Humanitarian reform, notably in penology and the antislavery movement, had as vigorous supporters in America as were to be found anywhere in Europe. European inspiration was freely acknowledged (especially John Howard in prison reform) but Americans were sufficiently independent to advance beyond their preceptors. The fertility of social invention displayed by the New World deeply impressed observant Europeans.

An awakened social conscience is one of the outstanding characteristics of the eighteenth century. In those years practical leaders, skilled in the ways of propaganda, shook indifferent parliaments and peoples into humanitarian activity. It was clear that human life was more highly valued in the New World than in the Old. The Quaker colony of Pennsylvania had probably the mildest criminal code in the Atlantic Civilization in the seventeenth century. The Quakers were associated with almost every phase of philanthropic activity. Though a relatively small group on both sides of the Atlantic, they were a conscience to the eighteenth century, and their voice rarely failed to cry out against injustice.

Legal Reform. Fundamental changes in the character of the laws did not come until after the epoch-making works of Montesquieu and Beccaria. Montesquieu's *L'Esprit des lois* argued that laws should be subjected to close examination to make them fit more properly the needs of society. Beccaria, in particular, was the inspiration for reformers everywhere, anxious to recast legal systems. A chief objective was the reform of antiquated codes relating to crime and punishment. It was the study of writings of European legal reformers by Jefferson which helped prepare the way for his own Virginia legislation on crimes and punishments. In a reversal of influences, Franklin gave strength to English and French reformers who argued against the injustice and unwisdom of capital punishment for minor crimes.

Penal Reform. Europeans were deeply interested in American prison practice, to which they generally awarded high praise. The results achieved in Philadelphia, particularly, were adjudged superior to European achievements. A French visitor, the Duc de La Rochefoucauld-Liancourt, paid eloquent tribute to the New World, calling upon her to reverse the process of borrowing "illumination" from Europe and to "serve in her turn as a model to reform the criminal jurisprudence and establish a new system of imprisonment in the old World." He recalled that the ideas were originally European, but "the attempt at an almost entire abolition of the punishment of death, and the substitution of a system of reason and justice, to that of bonds, ill treatment and arbitrary punishment, was never made but in America. (*See Reading No. 7.*)

Count Rumford, American Expatriate. Americans and Europeans exchanged ideas on life insurance, old age pensions, temperance, and proposals to eliminate duelling and poverty. The last question was attacked in a vigorous way by that versatile American expatriate, Benjamin Thompson, Count Rumford, who had entered the service of the Elector of Bavaria. He stimulated social improvements in many communities on the continent and in Great Britain by his example, his writings, and his earnestly solicited supervision.

Antislavery. Among the causes that appealed to humanitarians was the antislavery movement. Standing in the forefront of an international fellowship crusading against human bondage were Quakers on both sides of the Atlantic. Early in the eighteenth century they began to denounce slaveholding as unchristian, and not long after, started to disown fellow sectaries who persisted in holding slaves.

In both America and England during the Revolutionary era the argument against slavery as unchristian was bolstered by the familiar appeal of the individual's natural right to freedom. Granville Sharp, an English co-worker in all phases of humanitarianism, reminded Americans that many Negroes were natives of the colonies "and consequently have a *natural right* to a *free existence* therein, as well as the Landholders themselves."

Transatlantic Cooperation. It was the Philadelphia schoolmaster Anthony Benezet who was largely responsible for molding public opinion on the slave trade. His *Historical Account of Guinea* was credited by Thomas Clarkson, the great English leader in the cause, with doing more than any other publication to spread a knowledge and hatred of the trade.

The example of northern American states in abolishing slavery during the Revolutionary era was set up as worthy of emulation by European empires. It was believed that a universal abolition of the trade might be secured by treaty among interested powers, including France; for she, too, was the center of lively reform agitation. Emancipation by Quakers in Pennsylvania had stimulated the French to a discussion of this problem among themselves.

Humanitarians on both sides of the Atlantic marshaled evidence to controvert the argument that the Negro was an inferior being. American Friends wrote to English

coreligionists that Negroes were as capable as whites
when given the same advantages. Ethnological studies
were useful in refuting the view that there were different
species of man. Variations in climate, it was said, ex-
plained physical differences. It was pointed out that
Negroes and whites, too, had undergone physical changes
since their transplantation across the sea. Negro customs
of dress, marriage, and religion were compared with
those of western European society and found not inferior.

English Friends in the 1780's were writing optimistically
to America that people of all classes were now interested
in the movement against slavery. Optimism was short-
lived, however, for in the last few years of the century
reports from London were less enthusiastic. In a tone of
patient resignation the Pennsylvania Abolition Society
wrote to London that only gradual progress could be
hoped for.

Reform Eventually Prevails. On a test in the
British Parliament in 1792, a bill asking for the abolition
of the slave trade was defeated. British merchants and
planters opposed abolition, fearing it would give their
rivals in French Santo Domingo a superior competitive
position. Not until the early years of the nineteenth
century, after the French had lost their colony and when
British planters suffered from the effects of overproduction, could a prohibitory law by Parliament against the
slave trade be enacted.

Though the gains recorded by social reformers on
both sides of the Atlantic in the eighteenth century appear slight in retrospect because of progress made since,
to the people of that day the advances in humanitarian
endeavor were important. The mutual aid that reformers
on both sides of the ocean accorded one another was a
heartening demonstration of transatlantic cooperation.

— 3 —

SCIENTISTS AS "CITIZENS OF THE WHOLE WORLD"

Humanitarians erased geographical boundaries in their quest for social betterment. They were ably abetted by doctors, botanists, and other scientists who likewise ignored geographical limitations in creating their own "one world." Scientists perhaps more easily than others were able to transcend local boundaries and think of themselves as members of a fellowship bound together in a common search. The Royal Society in England was the dynamo that generated much of this activity, and it was a signal honor to be granted membership in it. A small number of colonials won the coveted position, and they made worthy contributions to the sum of knowledge accumulated by the Society. Careful observations on the habits of animals unfamiliar to Europeans, discovery of many new plants, closer study of the relationship between climate and disease—these were among the communications transmitted from America to England.

Scientists began writing in the vernacular instead of in Latin, thus reaching a larger audience. Scientific communications appeared in newspapers and almanacs, the latter reaching a circulation of many thousands in America

Botanists Cooperate. Natural science, notably botany, won particular attention in these decades. It is no coincidence that great progress should have been made in botany when a new floral world was being revealed to European investigators. The great botanists recognized their debt to investigators in the New World, and none with more graciousness than the most distinguished naturalist of them all, Linnaeus of Sweden. "We are all devoted to the love of exotic plants," he wrote, "especially those from America."

Men on both sides of the ocean were alive to the need for subsidized expeditions to America. Linnaeus suggested to the Royal Swedish Academy of Sciences that it send a botanist to North America to collect seeds of plants which would "improve the Swedish husbandry, gardening, manufactures, arts and sciences." The man chosen to go, Peter Kalm, not only published an interesting book on his travels in the colonies but also planted or distributed to others the seeds he had collected.

Expeditions came to America from Vienna and from Italy, but the most important was probably that from France. André Michaux came in 1785 to study trees for possible use in French naval construction. He traveled all over the country and sent back to France thousands of plants and many boxes of seeds. His son, François André, then only fifteen years old, started a long, fruitful career with this expedition. On three trips to the New World he gathered the materials for publications which are of major importance in the literature of America's natural history.

John Bartram. No American was held in higher esteem by European botanists than the self-taught Quaker John Bartram, who confessed quite simply, "I love Natural History dearly." The top men in his field in Europe were acquainted directly or indirectly with his work, which accounted for the introduction abroad of hundreds of new American specimens. Within less than half a century America, said Mark Catesby (1767), "has furnished England with a greater variety of trees than has been procured from all the other parts of the world for more than a thousand years past."

Other naturalists besides Bartram assisted European scientists, notably Dr. Alexander Garden of South Carolina (the gardenia is named after him) and John Mitchell of Virginia. Mitchell was one of the ablest scientists in America, laboring for years on a comprehensive natural and medical history of the colonies. William Bartram, the son of John, was a skilled naturalist who knew how to portray in words and colors the phenomena he met on his expeditions to remote regions. The Bartrams, father and son, made rich contributions to American literary tradition by writing about nature with authority and distinction.

Europe Plants American Trees. In several western European countries, declining timber supplies prompted experimentation with American trees. Englishmen planted the locust in large quantities for ships and rail fences. German foresters introduced fast-growing American trees to augment the dwindling supply of local timber. The rich variety to be found on aristocratic European estates owed much to America's bounty.

Agricultural Reform. The study and cultivation of flowers, trees, and shrubs satisfied esthetic as well as utilitarian needs. But husbandry was almost entirely a practical matter. The achievements of English agricultural reformers were revolutionary and the new ideas were disseminated throughout Britain and America. A signal British contribution to American agriculture was the improvement of breeds of livestock, while the French legacy was especially important in culture of the grape.

Arthur Young, editor of the *Annals of Agriculture* and chief preceptor of the new agriculture, had for his schoolroom America as well as the British Isles. Among the most eager of his disciples was George Washington, to whom Young sent English plows, various types of seeds, and advice on soil conservation.

Americans acknowledged the superiority of English husbandry, but they felt that they, too, were capable of aiding its progress, especially in the invention of agricultural machinery. Jefferson's mechanical ability, applied to agriculture especially, is well known. His most important achievement in this field was his invention of a new plow with a more efficient moldboard. The superiority of this device to existing implements was soon made known to progressive farmers in England. But it was an uphill struggle for the reformer. As in England, so in America, wrote one of them to Young, "Prejudices in favor of ancient modes are laid aside with difficulty."

Fascination of New Creatures. To the European in America none of the phenomena of nature was so stirring as the sight of new creatures. No European commentary was complete without reference to the beauty of the hummingbird or the fascinating horror of the rattlesnake. Overseas correspondents sent to the Royal Society their descriptions of American moose, pigeons, and whales.

The Study of Man. The study of man proved no less engrossing. One of the best works in anthropology by an American was the small volume by Samuel S. Smith of Princeton. His *Essay on the Causes of the Variety of Complexion and Figure in the Human Species* was quickly and favorably known abroad, where a British editor (1788) commended it for its dependable information on primitives. Smith showed how descendants of Europeans had changed in complexion and hair texture under the different climate of America. Whites who lived like Indians began to look like them. Negro field slaves, as contrasted with domestics, retained their African aspect longer. He concluded that if Negroes were free and participated equally in white society they would change their African physique and culture much faster.

Americans and Europeans became more critical in their approach to ethnological studies. Even popular works gave a more scientific view. Differences in environment and culture produce variations, said William Guthrie, author of a widely used geography, "but the great outlines of humanity are to be discerned among them all, notwithstanding the various shades which characterize nations and distinguish them from each other."

Franklin and Science. The history of scientific relations between Europe and America in the latter half of the eighteenth century can to a large extent be written around the personality of Franklin. He was better known abroad than at home, said the *Scots Magazine;* look in the foreign publications on electricity, it urged, where will be found on almost every page the terms Franklinism, Franklinist, and the Franklinian system. The article on electricity in the first edition of the *Encyclopedia Britannica* (1771) was largely dependent on Franklin's writings. He was, said an English biographer, the "American Newton." He was the only American whose reputation ranked him with the most eminent scientific figures of the day. It became the fashion to install lightning rods on houses though in America the fad grew more quickly than in Europe. For their easier installation Franklin drew up detailed instructions which were widely circulated in various periodicals. The Austrian Emperor put conductors upon gunpowder magazines, and Voltaire's example in putting a rod on his own house reassured the timid.

Americans in these years were not making many contributions of fundamental importance to science, but they did, in the manner of research assistants, supply some of the basic data. Probably the ablest scientist in America, and Newton's most distinguished disciple on this side of the Atlantic, was Professor John Winthrop of Harvard. His researches, made known to the Royal Society, of which he was a member, included papers on earthquakes and astronomy. Americans joined Europeans in two notable studies in astronomy, in 1761 and 1769. A consequence of this cooperative research was a more accurate determination of the distance from the earth to the sun.

Scientists as World Citizens.   Studies of wind and weather obviously had great usefulness in an age of sailing ships, and Americans joined enthusiastically in compiling the valuable data. Cooperative ventures of many kinds took place in the eighteenth century, reminding us once again of the international character of scientific fellowship. Dr. Benjamin Rush of Philadelphia understood it so when he wrote to that thoughtful English friend of America, Richard Price: "In science of every kind men should consider themselves as citizens of the whole world."

Medicine.   In few fields of science did Americans of the eighteenth century feel so much the equal of Europeans as in medicine. Medical education everywhere was of an uncertain character, more so in America, where (in 1776) only two hundred had medical degrees out of some three thousand individuals practicing medicine. Even in Europe a large proportion of physicians had gained their knowledge by a short apprenticeship to a doctor who also functioned as an apothecary.

Americans Study Abroad.   Americans felt that they had much to learn, and it was their good fortune to choose what was probably the best medical school in the world, Edinburgh. Americans continued to find it valuable for medical training in the twentieth century. The example of Edinburgh stimulated Americans to establish medical schools in their native land. They were fortunate, too, in having as their teacher in London John Hunter, who was credited with making surgery a real science. Very few American doctors in the latter half of the eighteenth century achieved distinction without some instruction in Europe or guidance from someone himself trained in a European school. It is also worth recording that some of the most distinguished doctors in eighteenth-century America were Europeans transplanted to the New World, among them being Drs. Alexander Garden, William Douglass, and Cadwallader Colden. And they brought along with their medical knowledge a general intellectual distinction to their overseas homes.

Benjamin Rush. From Philadelphia, the most important center of medicine in America, a large number of students carried the ideas of Benjamin Rush through the length and breadth of the United States. In a period of forty years after 1770, some three thousand students (counting apprentices and college pupils) learned their medicine from him. Americans who were familiar with medical training at home and in Britain soon began to write from England that medicine was "taught more scientifically in Philadelphia than in London." Nevertheless American resources were as yet inadequate for advanced training; there was not enough dissection and the variety of operations was limited.

American Contributions. While America was largely debtor to Europe for education in medicine, the balance was partly redressed by the free exchange of proposals for the advance of medical science. Americans had something original to say about epidemics and wrote wisely about fevers. They also shared their knowledge of medicinal plants with Europeans. The latter were told that very many roots, herbs, and barks used in America had been discovered by Indians, but that inexpert use by whites had made people discard them when they seemingly proved ineffective. In England early in the eighteenth century Joseph Addison had written in the *Spectator,* "We repair our bodies by the drugs from America."

Cooperation Against Smallpox. A very profitable result of the scientific relations between the colonies and England was the mutual encouragement offered in the adoption of inoculation against smallpox (deliberately injecting smallpox into an individual to heighten his immunity). Cotton Mather was the leading spirit in pressing physicians in the colonies and in England to undertake this method of fighting one of humanity's worst scourges. The practice of inoculation was more quickly adopted in America than in more conservative England.

Wherever the fight went on for inoculation, in England, France, Holland, Sweden, or elsewhere, Americans participated or their experience was drawn upon to support arguments for it. Within fifty years of Boston's adoption of inoculation in 1721 it had been introduced to most of Europe, and it soon became common to inoculate many people at a time.

At the end of the eighteenth century Americans were quick to see the superiority of Edward Jenner's practice of vaccinating with cowpox to immunize people against smallpox. Nowhere did Jenner find stronger support than in the United States. Benjamin Waterhouse of Massachusetts, "the American Jenner," was largely responsible for spreading a knowledge of vaccination throughout the United States. He remarked that the people of New England in 1721 had "set a noble example to their older brethren of Old-England. . . . Now the English in their turn lead the way in a practice still more salutiferous"; and he urged Americans to adopt it.

The problem of eradicating smallpox was the central one in transatlantic medical communications in the eighteenth century. The success that attended this American-European cooperative attack was a promise of greater victories to come in the general war against disease.

Community of Interest.   Americans who gladly sat at the feet of European masters in art or science felt that in politics they themselves were masters who could teach Europeans the facts of political life. This was especially true in the Revolutionary era when the War for Independence won an accolade from European liberals who were critical of their own antiquated political structures. The fraternity of believers in human progress lent encouragement to each other in the Atlantic world. The community of interest that was created in the last third of the eighteenth century among liberals everywhere in the Atlantic Civilization has been an enduring factor in the life of Western society even to our own time

AMERICA AND THE UTOPIAN IDEAL IN THE 18TH CENTURY

While Europeans sought from the New World gold and goods to increase their store, the greatest treasure they demanded from it was the fulfillment of an age-old dream of the ideal society. Grateful as they were to share in America's material bounty, they became petulant when she failed to live up to the dream that had been fashioned for her. In fact it was not unusual for America, at the very moment of lavishing her plenty upon an anxious Europe, to be warned lest her ideals be subverted in the pursuit of a universally desired wealth. Americans were expected to garner the fruits of the soil and the fish from the sea, but they were not to repeat the mistakes that common forebears had made in creating faulty civilizations. Migrants overseas were expected literally to begin the world again and on this new foundation to build the perfect society. Any deviation from the image created for them by a believing Europe did violence to Old World illusion. Despoilers of a dream are with difficulty forgiven.

America a Utopia. In man's long experience utopia had nearly always been in the past or the future. Rarely did it coincide with the present. But in the land beyond the western horizon Europeans had the striking good fortune to find their utopian dreams materializing.

In time America came to exist actively in the consciousness of Europe's masses—their dreams were almost all concerned with life in the New World. Letters from pioneer settlers, as well as books, pamphlets, articles, and personal accounts of returning travelers, all told Europeans of advantages overseas. Those who had found utopia were more vocal than those who had sought it in vain. In this blessed region the complications of Old World society vanished and there emerged a community of simple folk, men of nature, whom it pleased eighteenth-century philosophers to idealize.

Indians and Utopia. In recalling a sophisticated society to simplicity, the Indians played an important part. These "noble savages" were a guide to a new moral order, and the European's curiosity about them was insatiable. In the confused picture Europe had framed of the New World, "noble savages" embraced American-born white children who were spoken of as "tame Indians." The word American, in fact, to the ordinary European understanding, signified Indian. Writers found it necessary to emphasize the point that when referring to Americans, they did not mean Indians but rather descendants of European parents. American whites were said to have copied various customs from Indians which gave them a physical distinction matching the Greek ideal of beauty.

The American Image in Europe. In European minds the image of transatlantic peoples which evolved was that of a multiple Indian-Graeco-Roman-American personality. An English writer thus eulogized the capture of Louisburg (1745) by the colonials in the war against the French: "When I consider the coolness and bravery with which they marched to action, and their return from victory to their several occupations I take into my mind the great image of the ancient Romans leaving the plow for the field of battle, and retiring after their conquests to the plow again." Europeans were delighted with the rumor that the Olympic games might be revived in America. "All her friends wish it," wrote one of them, "and say they are capable of it, and having acted on Greek principles, should have Greek exercises."

Impact of the American Revolution. The vague aspirations of Europeans toward a new society were given solidity by the concrete appearance of the world of tomorrow in the thirteen colonies. England, Scotland, Ireland, France, Belgium, the German states, Holland, Scandinavia, and countries elsewhere in Europe and Latin America too—all these felt the currents from the western North Atlantic. John Adams was right when he said that a complete history of the American Revolution would be a "history of mankind during that epoch." Near the end of his long, rich life he told a correspondent that the

Revolution was no common event: "Its effects and consequences have already been awful over a great part of the Globe; And when and where are they to cease?"

"Stones of One Arch." Colonial revolutionaries were heartened by the response that came from well-wishers in nearly every country. English and American Whigs joined hands in opposition to the British administration. Great Britain and the colonies, they said, "must stand or fall together." Horne Tooke defended the American colonists in a political speech to fellow Englishmen: "The Security of their Freedom and their Rights is essential to the enjoyment of our own. We should never for a moment forget this important truth, that when the people of America are enslaved, we cannot be free; and they can never be enslaved whilst we continue free. We are stones of one arch."

Americans and their English supporters were in intimate contact during these years and continually reinvigorated each other. Their exchange of correspondence, their common understanding and warm sympathy account for the similarity in the organization and sentiments of radical associations on both sides of the Atlantic. The debt of each to the other is immeasurable. American propagandists, above all Franklin, kept the political pot a-boiling. Richard Price, John Cartwright, John Jebb, and many others wrote in behalf of the colonies. Cartwright, a life-long admirer of America, displayed the Declaration of Independence in a conspicuous position in his own home.

Zenger and Freedom of the Press. In the general struggle to broaden the area of freedom in the eighteenth century the movement for a freer press was of first importance. A strong impetus to free expression of opinion came from the famous Zenger case in New York. Many years after the event, courtrooms and legislative halls in England and America echoed the arguments of Andrew Hamilton in defense of John Peter Zenger, charged with publishing a criminal libel against the colonial governor. Zenger was acquitted and Hamilton's address to the jury became a classic on both sides of the Atlantic. Though many years passed before the principles for which Hamilton argued were incorporated into English law, a general relaxation in supervision of the press gradually came about. In England and elsewhere the American Revolutionary era loosened the official ties that had long restricted freedom of expression.

America and France. The close association between American and English radicals was only one of the threads that linked Europe's destiny with America. France, too, found support for a liberal position in American developments. French officers returning from the Revolution in America published accounts of the new country; and translations of travel books and histories of the states further served to spread a knowledge of America. Lafayette in particular was a most important medium through whom the American Revolutionary spirit was communicated to France.

Into a restless French society Franklin threw some elements that combined to make a turbulent mixture. It was one of Franklin's great honors, said Richard Price, that he had contributed much to bring on the Revolution in France. Jefferson's hold on French imagination was equally impressive; he was named "the apostle of the religion of liberty."

In the opinion of John Adams the American Revolution was possibly as influential in bringing on the revolution in France as were the writings of Diderot, Voltaire, and Rousseau. His view was supported by a contemporary German's admonition to those who were tracing the origins of the French Revolution to the writings of Rousseau and fellow *philosophes,* to remember the *acts* of the American Revolution and their stimulating suggestiveness.

New American state constitutions, especially Virginia's with its declaration of rights and its notable passages on tolerance and liberty, were translated for Frenchmen who were one day to write their own declaration of the rights of man. (*See Reading No. 8.*) It is important to remember that America was debtor as well as creditor to France, whose leading social philosophers, Montesquieu and Voltaire especially, were widely known overseas in American periodicals, colleges, and legislative halls.

America and Germany. German states were also brought within the orbit of American revolutionary influence. Young Germany saw in America a political utopia;

and some of her youthful writers thought to emigrate westward. In the works of Goethe, Lessing, and others, may be found enthusiastic expressions of interest in America. German magazines spoke of America as an escape for the disheartened and disinherited.

A fiery spirit burned bright in German poetry. In *Sturm und Drang,* whose scene is laid in America at the beginning of the Revolution, Klinger's hero cries, "Ah, let me but stand securely on American soil, where all is new." In *Die Freiheit Amerikas* (1783) Europeans were adjured to look to the model of American liberty now made secure. In America, said Christian Schubart, musician and poet, thirteen "golden gates are open to the victims of intolerance and despotism."

Friedrich L. Stolberg in *Die Zukunft* (1782) urged that not only should North America be free but South America as well. Would the Old World, he asked, then be content to remain in darkness? A very influential book of the period was *Über Nordamerika und Demokratie* (1782) by J. C. Schmohl. The author was not hostile to England, but he believed that America was destined to guide Europe out of political and social disintegration and bring it freedom.

America and Switzerland. In Switzerland public sentiment generally favored England, but a common thought was that Europe was about played out; in America would be found the future home of liberty. The historian, Johannes von Müller, who was lectured on America's destiny by an American friend, became convinced that his generation was standing on the divide between two ages. Abhorring violence and believing in the peaceful evolution of political institutions, he looked forward to the transformation of Great Britain and her colonies into a British commonwealth.

America and Italy. Italian patriots, too, found inspiration in the American struggle and in the writings of Franklin. A student of Franklin's influence in Italy writes that his "works and name passed from the library to the political assembly at the end of the eighteenth century." Philip Mazzei, friend of Jefferson, who wrote propaganda for the American cause in Paris and Florence, was certain that the vast mass of Italians were strong for

America; they "have called it aloud the *cause of mankind,* although they live under despotick governments."

Joel Barlow, the American poet and international adventurer, who played a role in Europe similar to that of Tom Paine, exhorted Italy to adopt French and American revolutionary principles. "Italy is destined to form one great republic," he prophesied. "The boundaries which nature has given it are peculiarly suited to this purpose." In free governments, he said, boundary questions can be settled without great difficulty as the United States has shown. Reports of the American Revolution were printed in Italian newspapers, and in Italy as everywhere, George Washington stirred the imagination.

America and Holland. In Holland John Adams was in close touch with Dutch patriots whose noted leader was J. D. Van der Capellen, a strong supporter of America. Adams discreetly made use of the Dutch press to advance his country's cause which was greatly benefited when the *Gazette de Leyde,* one of the most influential papers in Europe, threw its weight on the side of America.

America and Belgium. Conservative Belgium, (Austrian Netherlands) also felt the impact of new thought and action overseas. She caught the America fever largely through contact with Holland and France. The more important significance of America for Belgium came during the latter's own revolutionary period from 1787 to 1790. Europe's liberty, said Belgians, was at stake in the American fight for freedom. Coupled with the impetus supplied by France, transatlantic events were decisive in creating a revolutionary psychology in Belgium. Here, also, American heroes captured the imagination. Belgians were especially impressed by Washington's consistent refusal to use his position for personal aggrandizement.

Constitutions of American states were made known to the Belgians and were urged as a precedent in modifying provincial governments. Provinces announced their severance from the Habsburg Empire in a Declaration of Independence *à l'Américaine*. The manifesto of Flanders even repeated the very text of the American Declaration, and the Articles of Confederation were helpful to the Belgians in drawing up their own Treaty of Union. But, as happened to so many other budding plans all over Europe, the frosts of reaction delayed the ripening till well into the nineteenth century.

America and Ireland. No people were more deeply stirred by events in America than the Irish, whose difficulties with Parliament strikingly paralleled those of the colonies. All Ireland, said Horace Walpole, was "America mad." Irish resentment against England had an ancient history, but it was during the American Revolutionary era that programs for a change in imperial relations were more definitely formulated. Britain's new imperial policy after 1763 evoked the same response in Ireland as in America, for it was believed that coercion overseas was part of a more comprehensive, ominous plan which included Ireland as well.

In Ireland and in America, Hearts of Oak Boys and Hearts of Steel Boys effectively expressed hostility to the *status quo*. Irish readers kept track of the Sons of Liberty in America and counted the number of men in the colonies who were able to bear arms. It was hinted that civil war in America and in Ireland would be too much for the administration to bear.

When the colonies finally did engage in armed struggle, excitement in Ireland ran high. Her seaports gave shelter and supplies to American privateers. Irishmen boasted that their kinsmen in the American army were largely responsible for the defeat of the English at Saratoga. To wrest concessions from England, Irishmen adopted American techniques. They resolved to wear their own manufactures, and when shopkeepers were suspected of evading nonimportation agreements, they were, "after the American fashion," tarred and feathered.

Henry Grattan challenged the right of the British Parliament to make laws for Ireland. He summoned his fellow countrymen to rise to the dignity of statehood: "Before you decide on the practicability of being slaves forever look to America." And then in a warning to England he said, "What you trample on in Europe will sting you in America. When America sends forth her ambassadors . . . to Europe and manifests to the world her independency and power do you imagine you will persuade Ireland to be satisfied with an English Parliament making laws for her?"

Richard Price said all Ireland should continue to exert pressure on England, and he believed that Catholics should be given equal voting rights with Protestants as a way of breaking the hold of the aristocracy. To prevent any such collaboration between the two religious groups the laws against Catholics were considerably relaxed. In addition the Irish won important economic and political concessions, with autonomy for their own parliament. Well might Grattan say "the American war was the Irish harvest." But the harvest was followed by many lean years, and it was mainly the sustenance from America that kept alive the frustrated spirit of Ireland.

Dream of Equality. It seemed providential that a new land existed to receive those who would act on their dreams. And of dreams there were many. There was a dream of equality. Americans generally made a fetish of equality. As the *Encyclopedia Britannica* put it, "Every man thinks himself at least as good as his neighbor, and believes that all mankind are or ought to be equal."

Joel Barlow wrote in one of his studies addressed to a revolutionary Europe: "The word *people* in America has a different meaning from what it has in Europe. It there means the whole community, and comprehends every human creature; here [in Europe] it means something else, more difficult to define." That definition was made with considerable success by Thomas Pownall, a staunch friend of America in the British administration. He thus differentiated between European and American equality and liberty:

> Every Inhabitant of America is . . . equal in his essential . . . rights of the Individual to any other individual; is, in these rights, independent of any power that any other can assume over him; over his labour or his property; this is a Principle in act and deed, and not a mere speculative Theorem.
>
> The liberty of the People is not merely that share of Power, which an Aristocracy permits the People to amuse themselves with and which they are taught to call Liberty. It is not that share of Domination which a political Monarch throws into the hands of the

People, in order to ally their power to his Force, by which to govern the Aristocracy. The genuine Liberty on which America is founded is totally and intirely a New System of Things and men. . . . (*See Reading No. 9.*)

The "Poor Are Become Men." Crèvecœur's *Letters from an American Farmer,* widely circulated, strengthened the revolt against fate—man could will his own world. True, labor both free and bound had to face many hardships in the colonies, but the area of freedom available to it there was greater than in Europe. In America, Crèvecœur wrote in a noble phrase, the "poor are become men," and this metamorphosis resulted from their own laws and their own industry. The dignity of man depended not on artificial classification but on his inherent worth. German mercenaries who had fought in America were particularly impressed by this characteristic. (*See Reading No. 10.*)

Europe Fears American Equality. European governments feared the influence of those who had returned from America, for the latter frequently caused dissatisfaction at home and spurred emigration. Some travelers were emigration agents, and it quickly became clear that they, with their rosy accounts, were more successful in convincing people to undertake the journey to America than were agents who had never been overseas. These salesmen for America, working on a commission basis handling mainly indentured servants, were the most potent force in promoting emigration. Decrees were issued against their activities, but in one way or another they got the emigrants out.

In Switzerland, the canton of Berne feared an almost complete depopulation when emigration was especially great (1754-1770). Though restrictions were placed on emigration, few proposals were made to eradicate its causes. The use of undivided lands and of forests for the very poor was suggested in Switzerland. Prospective emigrants should be employed in new industries it was said, but there the matter rested. Though nothing much was achieved in ameliorating conditions for the lowly, the effect of emigration was to create a deeper concern with social problems.

Discontented Belgians who knew about cheap American lands circulated a pamphlet attacking Joseph II's policy hindering emigration. He was reminded that a happy, contented people needed no compulsion to stay at home; the unhappy would gravitate to wherever favorable conditions beckoned.

Emigration from Scotland. In Scotland, to quiet prospective emigrants, a few clan leaders relieved impoverished tenants at the expense of mortgagers and other creditors. Even so, large numbers continued to leave; and it was reported in the 1770's that landlords were forced to behave more circumspectly toward tenants. James Boswell, in the Hebrides in 1773, had been asked to join in a dance called "America," whose motif was the infectious nature of emigration. One resident told him that in the previous year, when a vessel left for America, relatives ashore waving good-by were "almost distracted." "This year," he wrote, "there was not a tear shed. The people on the shore seemed to think that they would soon follow. This indifference," concluded Boswell, "is a mortal sign for the country."

Pursuit of Happiness. In utopia life must be more secure, happier, and longer. English interest was quickened by fears of a steady depopulation at home. The statistics of population growth in America were well known to Europe, where it was argued that the American environment, with its longer life expectancy, was most favorable to mankind.

The pursuit of happiness had ended in its capture. At least so wrote a British publication: "It may in truth be said, that in no part of the world are the people happier . . . or more independent than the farmers in New England." A transplanted German in New Jersey expressed his joy: "The thought that the ground on which we and our children stand belongs to us, that our bodies are not the possession of a single individual and his whims, will always refresh with an inner satisfaction the European who comes here."

The quest for economic security seemed ended for those willing to work. America was no East Indies or Peru where wealth might easily be gathered, but "a very beautiful country" which guaranteed "to the industrious and ambitious worker a peaceful existence, a comfortable income, and an independent prosperity."

Higher Wages in America. British workmen heard of the high labor rates paid in the larger American cities. It is estimated that the real wages of a workman in America through much of the eighteenth century were from 30% to 100% more than the earnings of his contemporary in England.

Ministers in Scotland complained of the loss of many parishioners to America. And those who left sent money home to aid further emigration. Letters compared superior American conditions with Scottish demoralization, thus inciting more people to leave. Emigrants, when asked why they were going, generally answered "for Poverty and to get Bread," but Agnes Adair was probably not the only girl going to America "to find a husband." Scottish feudalism appeared starkly anachronistic when measured by American opportunities.

America the "Asylum" for the Oppressed. Time after time America was referred to as the "asylum" for the oppressed, a haven which seemed less appealing when reports reached Europe of disturbed conditions in the post-Revolutionary States. Warm-hearted Richard Price was among those who rejoiced when peace came and America's independence was assured. Her institutions, he told Franklin, were humanity's brightest star. He hoped American example would produce such a reformation in the English Parliament as to make it a *"real* representation instead of such a mockery and nuisance as it is [at] present." (*See Reading No. 11.*) The popular author Thomas Day said that the future association between Great Britain and the United States must be based on ties of friendship and mutual interest. The success of America, he asserted, was a great warning to the wielders of arbitrary power.

England's Freedom Linked with America's. The technique of arousing mass support for reform by forming committes of correspondence, etc., borrowed from America, was frequently resorted to in England at this time. Jebb, in urging this procedure, expressed the hope that "the acts of freemen on the other side of the Atlantic will inspire our countrymen on this with a similar spirit."

American independence, he believed, was an essential condition of freedom in England.

Utopians looked with an anxious eye upon Americans, who were troubled by many problems in the 1780's and exhorted them to hold fast to their ideals. Let the United States, wrote Pownall, "consider themselves as the means in the hands of Providence, of extending the Civilization of human Society. . . . If they take up this Character within themselves, and hold out its operations and effect to the Old World, they will become a Nation *to whom all Nations will come.*"

Richard Price Advises America. Price vigorously urged the creation of a federal government to decide disputes, regulate commerce, "to institute an union that shall have weight and credit," and gain the respect of Europe. Real power must be given to a central agency "without encroaching too much on the liberty and independence of the confederate states." Men like-minded with Price sought to warm hopes, chilled by contempt and indifference, at the American "flame of virtuous liberty."

Lessons America Taught the World. On the three hundredth anniversary of Columbus's discovery, Elhanan Winchester, an American then visiting in London, delivered an oration wherein he proudly listed the lessons his country had taught the world:

1. A large country could be ruled by a republican form of government without monarchy or an aristocracy.
2. Freedom of worship "is the best policy."
3. Church and state could subsist without alliance.
4. Milder punishment for crimes tends to prevent them.
5. People are happier and more contented under a "mild and equitable government," which is far stronger than arbitrary government and in less danger of being overturned.
6. America had also shown the world "that to admit the Jews to all the privileges of natural born subjects, is far from being a dangerous experiment, as has been generally supposed."

Jefferson's election and his inaugural address heartened the European liberal and gave opportunity to repeat the moral which taught that people were happier under mild and just governments. An Englishman remarked that the constitution of America was obviously "the most free one we know of; the Government of the New World is stronger, because juster, than any we witness in the Old." With this example Englishmen were urged to reform peacefully their own abuses.

In the decades immediately following the Revolution, and for long years thereafter, America counted heavily in the calculations of Englishmen. Radicals and anti-administration men were pro-American, while conservatives belittled the success of the new institutions arising overseas. Nevertheless, even conservatives took quiet pride in the American constitution modeled, they said, after England's unwritten one. Whatever was desirable in the Western Hemisphere was to be found only in the United States "which have derived from us both their character and constitution."

British Reformers Look to America.   In several important particulars American political wisdom was defended against the attacks of her detractors. Among the principal objects of reform in Britain were listed the representation of the people, the role of the national established church and the expenditure of public funds. In these respects, it was asserted, America had shown a praiseworthy superiority. It was estimated that a family of six in a European state paid in taxes about £ 17 annually; a family of the same size in America paid only 30 shillings. Yet in America, life, liberty, and property were just as secure. European inhabitants, unlike Americans it was observed, were generally *subjects,* not *citizens.* Emigration, it was argued, would serve to awaken European countries to a realization of the need for reforms.

America as a great experiment in social organization was a continual source of energy to the radical. Americans, said Joseph Priestley, the British scientist, went far beyond the Glorious Revolution of 1689: "they formed a *completely New Government* on the principles of equal liberty and the rights of man—without Nobles, without Bishops and without a King." Conservatives on the other hand were forced to reexamine their position to find new rationalizations of their privileges.

The movement for Parliamentary reform which had

antedated the American Revolution was intensely stimulated by it, but political change became part of a much broader program involving religious toleration, a free press, freedom of assembly, and free right of petition. Advocating an appeal to reason as against precedent, one writer said it was "not impossible that the nations of the earth would have been . . . sunk in apathy and ignorance" had not the American Revolution promoted a spirit of inquiry and discussion that made men long for freedom. The more radical reformers wanted universal suffrage and abolition of primogeniture, while individuals like Thomas Spence went even further to speak of the uselessness of an aristocracy to society.

Linking of Radicalism in the Atlantic Community. The interrelationship of American, British, and French radicalism preoccupied its spokesmen. American and French revolutionary symbols were embroidered onto the older British fabric. Citizen Lee, at the British Tree of Liberty, Haymarket, London, sold a pamphlet complaining of high prices and asking for a more representative Parliament. "This balance of power between the Rich and the Poor," it said, "would be productive of a thousand times more consolation to this Nation than the chimerical nonsense of court-jugglers, 'the balance of power in Europe.' " British publishers reprinted old publications on the American Revolution, adding new material on the French Revolution.

A recurrent theme stressed that America, Great Britain, and France must be in alliance for the freedom of humanity. Everywhere in the British Isles it was American and French inspiration that fired radical sentiment. "We ardently wish," said one, "the triple alliance (not of crowns but) of the *people* of America, France and Great Britain to give freedom to Europe and peace to the whole world."

In America support for the French Revolution during its first years was very vigorous. It is "but the first chapter of the history of European liberty," said Jefferson, who foresaw its wide effects. Radicals in Britain and America were revitalized and new groups were organized. As the American writer, Hugh M. Brackenridge expressed it, "If kings combine to support kings, why not republics to support republics?" In America it was feared that conquest of France would be followed by an attack from the victorious monarchies upon the United States.

Linking of Conservatives. Conservatives everywhere, of course, hated the French Revolution, especially after the first flush of general enthusiasm had passed. They disliked intensely celebrations favoring French revolutionaries. Distrust of France in revolution, shared by conservatives in both England and America, made for a tenuous bridge of understanding between them. The British Minister to the United States, George Hammond, was instructed to aid anti-Jacobin forces in America.

When John Adams succeeded Washington in an orderly election, even the skeptical in England seemed finally convinced that the merits in the American government were sufficient to promise it an enduring life. American hostility to France (later developments of the French Revolution altered earlier American friendship) warmed British hearts and made them see virtues where only shortly before they had seen defects. Arthur Young reminded gentlemen farmers that "as the danger of commotions increases in Europe, the eyes of mankind will necessarily be turned to the region [the United States] where Property remains respected." But at best it was a grudging acceptance by the ruling classes, for not very deep under the surface was the gnawing fear of America as a perpetual ideological threat and a potential economic rival to Europe.

Which Road Should Britain Walk? Upholders of conservative British traditions always remembered the disintegrating force of American Revolutionary ideology. America's political system, said a close observer, "did not fail to produce consequences momentous and calamitous to this country." Democratic principles, simple and intelligible even to the least educated, spread to Great Britain with incredible rapidity. The French Revolution further unsettled the political opinion of British people and gave currency to democratic ideals. "It is America, it is Paine, it is democracy, it is Jacobinism" which undermined Britain, cried the traditionalist. One conservative presented alternatives offered by his fellows down to the twentieth century: "whether we shall adhere to

British laws, British principles, British system, and the British Constitution; or whether we shall exchange these for the principles, the system and the constitution of the United States of America." Thus was baldly stated a fundamental factor in the evolution of the nineteenth century.

In the years when imperfect man dared believe in his perfectibility America made it seem less visionary. A Belgian liberal urged the adoption of the new political ideas in his own homeland, in his work *Représentants légitimes du Peuple.* One reader remarked that it portrayed Americans as the "wisest and most virtuous people of the world" and said that he seemed to see in it a modern version of Plato's *Republic* or More's *Utopia.* In later years, down through the nineteenth century, utopias under different names continued to be cherished. The Pantisocracy of Coleridge and Southey, Brook Farm of New Englanders, and the many utopian communities scattered over America poignantly revealed the craving of humanity to make its dreams come true.

— 5 —

THE NEW NATION AND THE "UNITED STATES OF EUROPE"

American Characteristics. In the middle and later years of the eighteenth century, Americans became more and more conscious of how different they were from Europeans. They believed their civilization to be unique, a new experiment in human relations. Their rate of growth, outstripping European countries, and their seeming security, protected by the Atlantic, gave them an almost overweening confidence in their future. Their boastfulness irritated Europeans, particularly England's ruling classes. The latter, reluctantly, were willing to grant Americans a special mechanical aptitude. A minor British official, assigned to the new Federal government, criticized American vanity which pretended to primacy in the arts, etc., but he added, "if they have any genius or original invention . . . it is in the mechanic arts." He insisted, however, that for the most part they copied English models.

American hustle and bustle, even if aimless, were already fixed in the national grain. On the other hand, Englishmen thought that Americans, at least in their forums, were direct and purposeful. A British publication, though giving the palm for oratory to the English, said that the debates in the Constitutional Convention showed that Americans "as men of business [and] speaking on a subject they thoroughly understand . . . are really more worthy of attention than the flowery speechifiers on this side of the water." Americans were certain they had a keener grasp of the essentials of political life than did Europeans.

Most foreigners who traveled in America were almost painfully aware of an insistent social equality. Comment was frequent on the rise to affluence of the lowly. A visiting clergyman praising America's beneficent laws, spoke of the practice of parents buying land for their children so that all might share equally; a parent would "shudder at the thought of making 5 children slaves or beggars for the sake of making the sixth a gentleman." At a time when English writers were saying that a fundamental condition for a prosperous state was "a large and solid basis of the lower classes of mankind" at the bottom of the social pyramid, a Yankee editor urged his readers to reject Europe's detestable maxim—"that the common people, who are three quarters of the world, must be kept in ignorance, that they may be slaves to the other quarter who live in magnificence."

American vs. European Civilization. Close contact with Europe reenforced American belief in the superiority of its civilization. From Madrid, John Jay wrote: "I never loved or admired America so much as since I left it." He was glad to learn that the anniversary of American Independence had been celebrated in Amsterdam: "If I am not much mistaken the time will come when that day will be considered as one of the most important in modern history." Americans, even those who had lived in England for a long time, artists and others, found it difficult indeed to take root. They had become aliens in a familiar world.

Jefferson thought that Americans did not sufficiently appreciate their blessings, which no other peoples enjoyed. He was willing to admit that Frenchmen were better mannered, and shone with especial distinction in the fine arts. He felt that Americans, however, were much happier than Europeans, the mass of whom faced a deplorable future.

Education in Europe and America. Like nearly every other institution, education came under close scrutiny in the Revolutionary era. So strong was the American nationalistic temper that foreign education even for advanced students was frowned upon. Plans for national education were drawn up by Rush, Nathaniel Chipman, and others. Republics to be long-lived, they said, must invest in popular education. Such states "are slow in discovering their interest, but when once they find it out they pursue it with vigor and perseverance." (*See Reading No. 12.*)

American civilization was held up as a possible stimulus to a new kind of schooling. This new education, it was proposed, should not be so exclusively concerned with study of wars and the intrigues of statesmen. It should deal rather with man in society and the development of the human mind. Richard Price said "the new world opened a new field for enquiry" and he hoped that as a result of these efforts and absence of all restraints on free discussion "the American Revolution will in the end prove the means of extending much farther than ever human investigation and improvement."

Ties between American and European education became much closer in the nineteenth and twentieth centuries. American financial aid to European institutions in these later years repaid something of the debt contracted in the colonial period. American students in large numbers went abroad, and a few Europeans began to enter American schools. It has been a story of mutual aid from the beginning and is one of the brightest chapters in the history of Western civilization.

Language and Nationalism. English booksellers were delighted at the prospect of an increased demand for their products from a growing population in America, but purists in speech were prophesying the day when the two countries would no longer have a common tongue. Those who opposed deviations from the mother tongue were helpless, for the generation after the Revolution was a period of great invention in the language spoken by Americans. Indeed, they had already referred to their tongue as the "American language."

The English language in America, enriched by additions from Indian, French, and Dutch sources, added words and expressions frowned upon by pundits, though occasional Americanisms were welcomed for their conciseness and vigor.

Although the language was changing from its parental stem, literature fashioned from it remained largely unchanged from English models. European critics scored Americans for their failure to root themselves at home; "till they shake off the trammels of Europe in poetry as well as European government, they will not rise above mediocrity."

Dramatists more quickly than others rooted themselves in the American scene. In the Revolutionary era practically every native play had realistic characters in plots based on current issues. Actors in certain roles were already endowed with the essential characteristics of the American—independence, directness of action, blunt speech, quick decision, a constant activity directed to practical ends, and a cheerful, rather obvious sense of humor.

Church and State in America and Europe. Escape from provincialism, so much sought after in letters, was more speedily achieved in religion. The struggle for religious toleration, and then for complete separation of church and state, took on added strength when it was tied in with the revolutionary thought of the latter half of the century. To British readers, especially Dissenters, New England was held up as superior to old England in matters that affected church and state. The open sympathy of English Dissenters for Americans during the Revolution was cause for bitter recrimination. New England, it was said, was "more the country of their hearts than the England wherein they were born and bred."

Though Europeans had long discussed relations between church and state, in the climate of the Revolutionary era the role of religion in society was more sharply defined. Europeans were immensely stimulated by the changes in American state constitutions, which severely limited established churches and provided for a greater degree of religious freedom than was generally the rule in their own lands. At the same time the loosening of rigid orthodoxy in European religious circles communicated its effects to Americans, contributing to the growth of deism. American deists such as Franklin and Jefferson, in common with European skeptics, read Hume, Voltaire, and other exponents of their "faith."

Europe and American Religious Toleration. Correspondents exchanged information about many details in the rapidly changing society of the closing eighteenth century. From Scotland came the query, "Are all sects equally regarded by your government, and equally eligible to civil offices? or is there any exception made with regard to Roman Catholics?" And from Princeton went the reply:

"There is no exception, and we find the Roman Catholics make zealous and attached citizens to the new states."

English Dissenters spoke glowingly of the Virginia act respecting religious liberty, and of the sixth article of the Federal Constitution stating that no religious tests were to be imposed for officeholders. Charles James Fox, speaking in Parliament for the repeal of the Corporation and Test Acts, called attention to the American example, "the imitation of which," he said, "would reflect the highest credit upon ourselves."

Broadening their appeal to include unprivileged Jews and Catholics as well, Dissenters now opposed toleration as too narrow a concept urging, rather, complete liberty as a right to be demanded, not as a privilege granted by the state. In this, the English had been anticipated by American nonconformists, who opposed any kind of religious establishment.

It was Richard Price, America's devoted friend, who did much to spread news of religious developments in the States. His enthusiasm for Virginia's famed act was unbounded: "It is the first of the kind that was ever pass'd," he told Rush, and it was a "happy omen of the benefit to mankind that may arise from the American Revolution."

Jefferson proudly wrote to his colleague Madison that Virginia's act for religious freedom, widely translated, had been enthusiastically received in Europe, not by governments, he said, "but by the individuals who compose them." "It is honorable for us to have produced the first legislature who had the courage to declare that the reason of man may be trusted with the formation of his own opinions."

Toleration in the Atlantic Community. Europe expected much from Americans who had advantages the Old World had never granted. America had Europe's experiences to build on and, it was hoped, the wisdom to avoid her follies. It has been a long, never-ending process, this mutual civilizing of Americans and Europeans. They have on many occasions aided each other in living up to their common ideals. Americans were proud of their example of peace amid religious diversity, and felt they did have much to teach the world, though they were not averse to sitting at Europe's feet. The enlightenment, originating in Europe, severed some from a religious life; but for many it gave a broader basis to religious thought and observance. The limits of the City of God were measurably widened by the builders of the Atlantic Civilization.

Europe Fears America's Economic Power. The heritage of the Revolutionary years left bitter memories in England and America, although manifestations of friendliness persisted which were a countertheme to the dominant note of hostility. Americans and Europeans have looked at each other with mingled hope and fear since the eighteenth century. England, in particular, was concerned with America's future economic power. It was widely believed that the United States would be a formidable economic rival to Old World countries. "All Europe will feel the shock," it was prophesied, "and her power and consequence must naturally dwindle as those of America shall rise."

To prevent the growth of the New World it was suggested that America be partitioned and controlled by European powers. A different point of view was expressed by a scholar friendly to the United States. With remarkable prescience, Professor E. A. Zimmerman said that America would be a vast storehouse always ready to spread its largess over Europe's penury.

Anglo-American Reconciliation. The Revolution was looked upon by many in England and America as a civil war, and it was believed that a reconciliation might be effected even though each branch of the empire was now an independent unit. David Hartley devoted years in and out of Parliament to the furtherance of Anglo-American friendship. Included in the broad imperial outline he favored was the grant of virtual dominion status to Ireland. He had suggested the same for the colonies during the Revolution, and even after 1783 he continued to think in terms of an Anglo-American alliance based on commercial reciprocity and strengthened by common culture and traditions. Canada, he believed, was a common factor of interest; and so it has proved to be in the creation of the North Atlantic triangle.

Prophecies of American Supremacy. More than a few Englishmen were impressed by the tremendous re-

sources of the United States, for which an imperial role
was forecast in the Caribbean and in South America. It
was the belief of many that America was to be the new
base of empire, with the center of gravity in the Atlantic
community shifting to the New World.

Bishop Berkeley's belief in the westward movement of
empire had numerous supporters. Turgot prophesied that
separation of the colonies from England would be followed by separation of all America from Europe. It was
also thought that ease of escape for Europeans from bad
governments would force their rulers to adopt more enlightened policies. The Abbé Galiani of Naples, long a
partisan of Americans, said that the Revolution would
decide whether America was to rule over Europe or the
latter was to continue ruling over America. He was wager-
ing in favor of America.

Another clergyman, the Abbé Grégoire, said that the
United States would "change the face of the commercial
world and the face of empires." "Who knows," he asked,
"if America will not then avenge the outrages she has
received and if our old Europe, placed in the rank of a
subaltern power, will not become a colony of the New
World?" Horace Walpole, writing in the month of America's Declaration of Independence, suggested that the
little island of England would someday look back proudly
to "its former brave days, and swear its capital was once
as big as Paris, or—what is to be the name of the city that
will then give laws to Europe—New York or Philadelphia?" (*See Reading No. 13.*)

The Atlantic Alliance. Thomas Pownall, in his
perceptive *Memorial Addressed to the Sovereigns of
Europe and the Atlantic* (1783) told his readers that "the
peculiar orbit of every planet of the European system is
disturbed, and the center of the general system of Europe
is shifted." He called for a "real family compact" between
the two Atlantic powers, Great Britain and the United
States, urging the creation of a "great marine Atlantic
Alliance." George Canning's action, leading to the issu-
ance of the Monroe Doctrine, was foreshadowed in
Pownall's plea that England and the United States join
in opening up South America to commerce for all the
world. (*See Reading No. 14.*)

Plans for World Peace. Many of the leading men in the eighteenth century had a vision of world peace to be achieved by some supranational organization. Franklin confided to Richard Price, in the midst of the Revolution, his hope for a plan "that would induce & oblige Nations to settle their Disputes without first Cutting one another's Throats." Dr. John Fothergill, noted Quaker physician in London, wrote to Franklin about a college of justice where the claims of sovereigns could be weighed and war would then be levied only on those who refused submission to its decrees.

America's Example and European Unity. Franklin was quick to suggest the example of the federated American states of 1787 to Europe's notice. He believed that its success would spur Europe to carry out the "Grand Design" of Henry IV and his minister, Sully, by forming a federal union of its different states and kingdoms. The peaceful settlement of boundary disputes between American states prompted Robert R. Livingston to write Lafayette: "The day will come when all disputes in the great republic of Europe will be tried in the same way, and America be quoted to exemplify the wisdom of the measure."

Washington told Lafayette that America had sowed "seeds of Liberty and Union that will spring up everywhere upon earth. Some day, taking its pattern from the United States, there will be founded the United States of Europe." Frenchmen and Englishmen were already calling for a constitution for a proposed United States of Europe.

It is a tribute to the persistent vitality of America that even though she often strayed from her own ideals, she continued to fertilize the imaginative life of mankind. To millions she brought sustenance for the body and spirit. She gave modern man a real foundation for his utopian fantasy. In the many decades since independence, Americans and Europeans have been struggling to understand each other. Anti-Americanism has been matched by anti-Europeanism; the latter in its more virulent form has been mainly Anglophobia. Fundamental economic and political conflicts created deep fissures in the Atlantic world, and only in our own day, after infinite suffering, has a partial unity been achieved.

America Inspires Nationalism and Federalism.
America inspired the growth of nationalism all over the
world; the blow that the Declaration of Independence gave
to colonialism reverberates to our own day. But the growth
of nationalism was partly offset by the impetus American
federalism gave to plans for regional and world organization. The creation of a federal government apparently
accommodating differences between antagonistic states
gave a more solid foundation for the dreams of European
federalists, who had cherished such hopes for centuries.
America's mixed population merging into a homogeneous
unity was an example with constant appeal to philosophers
and the unlettered alike.

Men with a world view, in Europe and America,
favored some sort of association of nations whose task
would be to build the international community. It is a
striking challenge that these visionaries in the American
Revolutionary era flung at mankind. Our world is now
striving to give substance to those visions. It is easy to
believe that Franklin and his contemporaries would have
considered America the logical setting for a United Nations home.

— 6 —

THE ATLANTIC CIVILIZATION
IN THE 19TH CENTURY

In the eighteenth century it seemed that Europe was
more conscious of America than the colonies were of the
Old World. In the era of the French Revolution and
Napoleon the relationship was reversed and America
seemed to be more conscious of Europe than the Old
World was of the New. Political parties in the newly established Federal government were identified by their par-
tiality for France (Republicans) or England (Federalists).
The once stimulating and quotable Voltaire was banished

for his irreligion and social subversion. In the fearful imaginings of conservatives the now satanic figure of Tom Paine dominated the scene. John Adams, writing to a friend in 1805, thought that no man in the world had equaled him in influence over a period of thirty years; "Call it," he said disparagingly, "the Age of Paine."

The nations of Europe, engaged as they were, first in the conflicts of ideas precipitated by the French Revolution, and then in the conflict of arms, were not greatly concerned over America. True, they sought her food and other supplies, but she was not in these years pressing hard on the consciousness of Europeans. In the calculation of great powers the United States was of low rank. Indeed, like all lands outside Europe, she was considered too unimportant to affect deeply the decisions of the mighty. Closing of the seas to easy emigration in this period limited contacts of the masses of people with America, and thus a force which in former years had acted powerfully on their imaginations lost much of its strength.

While the lines of communication between the United States and Europe seemed less firm than formerly, other areas of the world began to impinge more strongly on the American consciousness. Trade in the Mediterranean brought contact with North Africa, not always pleasant when Barbary pirates exacted tribute. Ships of Salem and neighboring ports made the long run to China's coast, bringing back with them to New England something of the art and mystery that was Asia. Nearer home, in the ports of South America, increasing numbers of Yankee ships suggested the resourcefulness of North American merchants, always ready to seek new avenues of trade.

The Continuing American Revolution: In Latin America. It was, in fact, in South America that the shock wave of the American Revolution rolled on in the early years of the nineteenth century. Madrid, even during the American Revolution, though aiding the colonial revolt, had feared that successful rebellion of the British colonies might become epidemic in the nineteenth century. England and her former colonies, it was predicted, would effect a rapprochement and together they would erode Spain's empire. In signing the treaty which made America free, said the Abbé de Pradt, "Europe signed the great charter of emancipation for all the colonies."

There had been economic and cultural contacts between Latin America and the Anglo-American colonies from early years. When Spain opened her colonies to neutral trade in 1797, the United States became the chief beneficiary. All told, United States exports to Spanish America in the decade after 1796 grew from 3% to 12% of her total export trade. Latin American ports, it should be noted, were a valuable way station for United States ships going to China and the East Indies.

In the years following the American Revolution a growing uneasiness to the southward indicated the probable fulfillment of earlier prophecies—that all the Western Hemisphere would throw off its allegiance to Europe. New England merchants trading to Latin America carried with the usual wares copies of the Declaration of Independence in Spanish, along with federal and state constitutions. William Shaler of Bridgeport, Connecticut, made a career of spreading republicanism throughout the Spanish Empire, as he passed through México, California, and Cuba, the last of which he urged to throw in its lot with the United States.

Miranda and Fellow Atlantic Revolutionaries. Toward the end of the eighteenth century Francis Miranda of Venezuela, participant in the American Revolution, the French Revolution, and the War for Liberation of South America, was in touch with men who had carried the American Revolution through to completion and were anxious to see the colonies of Spain follow in their footsteps. From North America, Miranda went to England, where he lodged with Joel Barlow; and his coming prompted a newspaper to speak of the flames of revolution spreading from the United States to the Spanish Indies.

In England Miranda met people like Pownall who urged expansion of Anglo-American influence in Latin America. Pownall discussed (1790) with William Pitt a joint Anglo-American project to revolutionize South America and open its commerce to the English-speaking peoples. As time passed, Miranda came to doubt the willingness of the United States to aid his plans, and his hopes for foreign support were transferred to revolutionary France. Her example, he believed, would be followed by his own South America. In France, Miranda was part of a circle which included Barlow, Brissot, and Tom Paine, thus linking the revolutionary aspirations of the whole Atlantic world.

Miranda's travels in search of sponsors of revolution brought him back to the United States. He dined with Jefferson, who in speaking of Spain's insurgent colonies said (October 1808) "We consider their interests and ours as the same, and that the object of both must be to exclude all European influence from this hemisphere." The notion of solidarity among peoples of the Western Hemisphere, whose governments were to be based on liberal republican institutions in contrast to Europe's absolutism, was an idea that began to gain much strength even before the Monroe Doctrine gave it official status. Miranda, never tiring, finally did mount an attack on Venezuela (which was really a joint Anglo-American enterprise), that proved a vain venture.

The time for Latin American independence was not yet, but quickly, dramatically, it ripened. Napoleon's closing of Europe to Britain's trade turned British thoughts more actively to Latin America. The London *Times* (January 9, 1808) spoke of Spain's colonies as ready to fall from the parent stem; "as all Europe is now enslaved, it may be better for us to have free states, than dependent ones in the rest of the world." But Spain's uprising against Napoleon altered clandestine plans to revolutionize her colonies. Instead, England and Spain now effected a rapprochement, and a damper was placed on Miranda's activities by the British government.

Independence of Latin America. In the midst of Spain's conflict with Napoleon her American colonies declared their independence. The fledgling states debated the forms of government they should adopt, and copying of the example of their North American neighbor was promptly urged. Some pleaded for a United States of Mexico and a United States of South America. It was argued that extent of territory is no obstacle to union, "if a free and representative plan is adopted." It was precursors of Miranda's type who communicated to others the zeal for South America's independence which was soon to be realized.

The United States and Latin America. It was at this time (about 1810) that cultural and commercial contacts between North and South America increased markedly. In the two decades after 1810 the United States seems to have "discovered" Latin America. She already had a considerable stake in Latin America and her expectations were even greater. Ships from Baltimore, Salem, and other American ports were beginning to call more frequently at Montevideo and Buenos Aires. The persistent expansionist aims of the United States combined with revolutionary principles to keep stirring the native pool of discontent in South America.

In "liberating" Spain's possessions, Hamilton, Aaron Burr, Rufus King, and others sought either to gratify personal ambition or to extend the frontiers of the United States into Texas, Florida, and Cuba. American interest in Cuba has a long history. By agreement with Britain (1797) the United States was to take Havana, and together the Anglo-American forces were to subsidize revolution in Latin America. For a generation thereafter the English-speaking powers warily watched each other's moves in Cuba, whose location gave it a commanding position in the trade of the Caribbean world.

Americans were not of one mind respecting the Spanish colonies. Federalists looked with jaundiced eye on revolts there. Jeffersonian Republicans, on the other hand, were inclined to befriend the cause of the rebels. President Madison and Congress looked benevolently on their revolutionary aspirations.

These aspirations were nurtured from many sources. Britain encouraged free trade, France sent revolutionary doctrines winging across the Atlantic, Spain's liberalism, frustrated at home, came to fruition among followers in the colonies. But the United States was a working experiment in government which seemed to have especial meaning for South American revolutionaries. For them, as for Europeans, Washington, Jefferson, and Franklin became familiar names.

America and Chile. In Chile, through two men the influence of America made itself strongly felt in the course of revolutionary events. Joel R. Poinsett, a far-ranging American, speaking Spanish, carried the banner of revolution to Chile, where as consul he intertwined it with that country's flag. Camilo Enriquez, his close friend there, a liberal friar and journalist, was an ardent disciple of America's revolutionary leaders, who, he declared, had established "the beacon which we should follow."

Rivalries of Atlantic Powers in Latin America. In the decade after Napoleon's fall the Atlantic world's involvement in the dissolving Spanish empire became very complex. Spain sought Great Britain's aid, and France's too, against the territorial ambitions of the United States, but with no success. France on the other hand, in an attempt to block British economic expansion in South America, promoted friendship with the United States, then Britain's leading maritime rival. The French Abbé de Pradt had a sharp awareness of Europe's relation to Latin America. He favored the intervention of European powers in behalf of Spanish American independence, believing that this would tie Latin America to Europe. Latin America, he said, was Europe's frontier in the New World, and Old World intervention would insulate this bastion against the pull of America's revolutionary magnetism. The Old World was fearful that a republican New World, led by the United States, would constantly endanger monarchical Europe.

American Policy Hesitant. The United States government wavering between friendly endorsement of rebel aims and "correct" relations with Spain, was being pushed by various pressures into more open support of revolutionary regimes. Partisans of the rebels became more outspoken in the United States. H. M. Brackenridge, in "A Letter to James Monroe" (1817) said his country should be the first to recognize the new states, thus gaining commercial and ideological advantage. Like others in these years who anticipated the Monroe Doctrine, Brackenridge spoke of the United States as the natural leader of the Western Hemisphere, whose two continents were bound together by common interests to oppose the Old World.

Anglo-American Cooperation in Latin America. In keeping with older proposals of Thomas Pownall, an unofficial Anglo-American alliance supplied arms and ships to rebels, and their privateers swept Spanish royalists from nearby waters. Mathew Lyon, a New England politician, spoke (1816) of "Anglo-Americanizing" South America, whose revolt was widely recognized to be "the greatest event of the age for the whole Atlantic world." A Yankee adventurer, David Curtis DeForest, backed by merchants in Baltimore, New England, and New York, won a fortune through smuggling and privateering, and fame through support of Latin American independence.

The press, Congress, pamphlets, books, the agitation of South American agents, and the direct action of numerous adventurers all built up a powerful pressure for United States recognition of the new republics. There could be no doubt, said Henry Clay, that Spanish America "once independent will be animated by an American feeling and guided by an American policy. They will obey the laws of the system of the new world, of which they will compose a part in contradistinction to that of Europe."

Disillusionment with the behavior of rebel governments in Latin America tending toward authoritarianism moderated earlier enthusiasm in the United States. Jefferson himself began to be skeptical about their capacity for self-rule, but he did say "In whatever governments they end, they will be *American* governments, no longer to be involved in the never-ceasing broils of Europe. . . . America has a hemisphere to itself. It must have a separate system of interests which must not be subordinated to those of Europe."

Other voices reminded Americans that their commercial and political relations with South America were far less important than those with Europe. Overtones of Anglo-Saxon racial superiority also marked conservative opposition to interference in this alien struggle. Anxiety lest negotiations with Spain over Florida be endangered likewise contributed to dampening American interest in the fortunes of South American republics.

United States and Latin American Independence. When, after tortuous diplomacy, Spain ratified the treaty (1819) which added Florida to the United States, the way was open to recognizing the independence of the South American states. The way was made easier by a succession of disasters in 1821 to Spain's efforts to hold on to her dwindling empire. Peru, Venezuela, and Mexico all seemed finally lost. Remaining doubts as to the wisdom of American recognition were resolved.

Revolution in Spain itself in 1820, begun among expeditionary forces assembled to reconquer lost colonies, was instigated in part by agents from South America's new governments. The course of events stemming from this revolt eventually changed the alignment of European powers and relationships in the Atlantic world. Fear was general that the Holy Alliance might crush free governments everywhere, starting in Europe and possibly extending its talons to the New World.

A mixture of motives had at length brought recognition of rebel South American states—a genuine desire to encourage the spread of republican institutions in Latin America as everywhere else, American territorial expansion, and the hopes of businessmen that new markets would be opened in the freer trading area of an independent South America. The drive to best Britain in the race for commercial supremacy also played its part in bringing about recognition of the new states.

Britain Fears a Transatlantic League of North and South Americans.   On the other hand, fear of American initiative forced Britain along the road to recognition. "It is obviously the policy of the United States," said George Canning, "to connect itself with all the powers of America in a general Transatlantic League, of which it would have the sole direction. I need only say, how inconvenient such an ascendancy may be in time of peace, and how formidable in case of war." Finally the victories won by Bolívar and San Martín over Spanish royal forces sealed the doom of the once great empire and made recognition by North America of successor states inevitable.

The Monroe Doctrine and Europe.   The creation of republics in the Western Hemisphere was, as Tom Paine wished it to be, a great blow to monarchical power. The message of Monroe, which espoused republicanism for the New World, was a challenge to royalty in the Old. The Monroe Doctrine had revolutionary implications for the Old World which its masters were quick to perceive. In January 1824 the Austrian chancellor, Metternich, wrote to Nesselrode, the Russian minister: "These United

States of America which we have seen arise and grow . . .
have suddenly left a sphere too narrow for their ambition,
and have astonished Europe by a new act of revolt, more
unprovoked, fully as audacious, and no less dangerous
than the former. They have distinctly and clearly announced their intention to set power against power . . .
they have cast blame and scorn on the institutions of
Europe most worthy of respect. . . . In fostering revolutions wherever they show themselves . . . they lend new
strength to the apostles of sedition and reanimate the
courage of every conspirator." But Lafayette still was
America's champion. Monroe's message, he said, was
"the best little bit of paper that God had ever permitted
any man to give to the world."

America and the Greek Revolt. Wherever the
tinder of revolt was gathered America sparked it into
flame. Shortly before his death in 1826, Jefferson once
more bequeathed the Declaration and July 4 to posterity.
"May it be to the world . . . the signal of arousing men
to burst [their] chains . . . and to assume the blessings
and security of self-government. . . . All eyes are opened,
or opening to the rights of man. . . . There are grounds
of hope for others."

In America and in other Western lands, the Greeks
found support for their struggle against the Turks. Lord
Byron, who had always been aware of the impact of the
American Revolution on the world, went to help the
Greeks in their war for independence. He began his
journal in Greece with these lines:

> The dead have been awakened—shall I sleep?
>   The World's at war with tyrants—shall I crouch?
> The harvest's ripe—and shall I pause to reap?
>   I slumber not; the thorn is in my couch;
> Each day a trumpet soundeth in mine ear,
>   Its echo in my heart—

Meeting were held all over the United States in the
1820's to raise funds for Greek revolutionaries and to
extend to them America's sympathy. Youthful Americans
revering the ancient Greek inheritance fought by the side
of modern Greeks whose behavior sometimes disenchanted
their supporters.

Enchanted Americans, like Edward Everett, fervently spoke in behalf of the Greek cause and kept in close touch with leaders of the revolt. It flattered Americans to learn that the constitution drawn up by Greek revolutionaries (1822) was modeled after that of the United States, a republican form of government granting religious toleration and freedom of the press. Webster made a mighty appeal in 1824 for official recognition of the Greek rebel state, but the United States government preferred caution to sentiment. Not until 1833, when the great powers of Europe had established a guardianship over the new Greek state, was recognition given to it by the United States.

America and Russian Radicals. America lent her support to radicals in other lands of eastern Europe. Alexander Radischev, an enlightened Russian aristocrat, coupled Cromwell and Washington in his *Ode to Freedom* which hailed the American Revolution. Radischev, writing in the 1780's was especially conscious of the relationship between America's liberty and her free press. His writings were a continuing support for the aspirations of Russian revolutionaries in the nineteenth and twentieth centuries.

Russian reformers, planning a new structure for their motherland, drew inspiration from western Europe and America. The Decembrists of the 1820's were strongly influenced by American constitutionalism, and their plans for a Russian federal government suggested imitation of America's example. For a hundred years the American form of federalism was a lamp to light the path of Russian underground federalism. One of the early constitutional projects even divided Russia into thirteen states, a clear instance of Americanism in Russian political thought.

Alexander Herzen, in particular, was susceptible to the influence of America. Her future was great, he said, and her democratic vigor would cause her to outstrip western Europe. The latter declined rapidly in his estimation after the ill-omened days of 1848, which prompted him to say that henceforward western Europe was dead. For a renewal of society, said Herzen, there remained only two sources—America and eastern barbarism. It is the world's sorrow that Russia chose much of the latter.

America vs. Russia. It was not uncommon in mid-nineteenth century to oppose the brightness of America to the threatening darkness of Russia. Tocqueville spoke of the United States as the future champion of Western ideas of liberty in conflict with Russia. The Crimean War spurred talk of Anglo-American defense of the values of Western civilization. Though Englishmen knew of the American tradition against European entanglements, they could not refrain from saying that "when Cossackism has established itself on the shores of the Atlantic, it will be too late to discuss the *policy* of intervention, too late to take the initiative." (*See Reading No. 15.*)

Kossuth on America. When Louis Kossuth was seeking aid in the United States for his Hungarian revolution he spoke to an audience in Plymouth, Massachusetts: "While the tree of freedom which the Pilgrims planted grew so high that a twig of it may revive a world, in Europe, by a strange contradiction, another tree has grown in the same time—the tree of evil and despotism. It is Russia. Both have grown so large that there is no more place for them both on earth. One must be lopped, that the other may still spread."

The ties between the American Republic and northern and western Europe were intimate and of lasting consequence for the civilization of the North Atlantic. For Europeans, as John Adams had prophesied, the American Revolution was a continuing event. It was an ideological Gulf Stream warming the hopes of reformers and thawing Europe's frozen class structure.

America and Scandinavia. The countries of Scandinavia, too, came under this warming influence. Swedish aristocratic liberals in 1809 in opposition to absolutism planned their own version of America's Congress, but were defeated by upholders of the traditional Riksdag with its four estates. In Norway, Judge C. M. Falsen, the father of the Norwegian constitution (1814), named his son George Benjamin in honor of Washington and Franklin. Norway's constitution showed that its makers were familiar with American state constitutions and the Federal Constitution.

America and Belgium. A prominent leader in the drawing up of Belgium's constitution of 1830, Désiré de Haerne, spoke proudly of his country's emulation of

America's liberal institutions. After careful consideration, he said, America's example was thought superior to England's in all that related to public liberty, the distribution of power, the election of representatives, and decentralization of rule. De Haerne, a liberal Catholic priest mindful of America's leadership in separating church and state, argued successfully for adoption of this principle in the Belgian national congress. His was the first country in Europe to adopt this radical innovation.

America and Germany. German interest in the American experiment was of long standing. Her poets and political philosophers continued to find America a subject for rhapsody, while German businessmen sought to expand trade with the New World. Very progressive commercial treaties were arranged between the United States and Prussia in the late years of the eighteenth century and again in 1828. Emigrants from the continent to the United States usually passed through Hamburg and Bremen. These cities were especially prominent in Europe's commerce with America, Bremen concentrating on the importation of tobacco from the United States. A leading personality in promoting German-American economic ties was Friedrich List. List, emigrating from Germany, had been in the United States for some time before becoming American consular representative in Leipzig in 1832. He was strongly influenced by Hamilton's ideas and vigorously promoted trade protection for the German states.

The American political system had an especial appeal for Germans, who in the generation after Napoleon were in continual debate about the best form of government for themselves. The American federal system was a constant inspiration for German federalists. In numerous pamphlets they publicized the advantages of this political structure. In the Frankfort Assembly (1848), gathered to draw up a new constitution, America's influence was most clearly marked. The United States Constitution was studied as a model, and many of its provisions were incorporated into the document drawn up by the Assembly. The government created at Frankfort was immediately recognized by the United States, which believed that German liberalism was in close accord with New World principles.

But the dreams of Teutonic liberals themselves still submissive to authority vanished in the harsh reality of Bismarck's Germany.

America and Italy. Italian republicans and advocates of federation in the peninsula admired America's example. Luigi Angeloni in his *Italy at the End of 1818* proposed a federation copied directly from the United States. Federalists reminded rival proponents of a unitary state that Italy had to provide for local traditions and provincial interests. "We also want unity," they said, "but . . . the unity of the United States of America, not that of . . . Russia crushing Poland."

Mazzini, though rejecting America's federal example for a future Italian state, did find much that was inspiring in New World experience. He thought worthy of imitation America's Constitutional Convention; he praised United States opposition to secret diplomacy; he thought worthy of emulation guerrilla revolutionary warfare. Like others of his generation he thought America's mission was to teach republicanism to the world.

Mazzini was grateful for support from the small groups of Italians scattered over the United States. No American became so deeply involved in Mazzini's revolutionary cause as did Margaret Fuller. Distinguished writer and crusader in many good causes, she sacrificed everything for Young Italy. She cared for the wounded in the besieged Roman Republic (1849) and trumpeted to the world her belief in Mazzini's greatness. But that Republic was doomed to be extinguished by the France of Louis Napoleon allied with Spain, Austria, and Naples. Out of the disaster came the realization that success for revolutionaries on the continent could be won only if a "Holy Alliance of the People" could be organized in opposition to the "Holy Alliance of the Despots."

Mazzini on America's Mission. The far-ranging talk of the Young Americans in the middle of the century to "republicanize" Europe lifted Mazzini's hopes once again, but the quick eclipse of this brash group in the United States darkened for him the light in the western sky. Though Mazzini derived little practical aid from the United States, he kept alive his belief in America's destiny. To an American correspondent he spoke his faith: "With a sum of force almost fabulous in energy unknown to our monarchies . . . you have impressed in the heart of Europe the conviction that in you abides a force, a power almost incalculable, at the service of human progress. . . . You must manfully aid morally, and if necessary, materially your republican brethren everywhere the sacred battle is fought. . . . This is your mission, this is your glory and safety; this is your future!"

France and America. The French took a proprietary interest in the United States, as though they had hatched the fledgling republic. They were very conscious of their contribution to American independence and watched closely the growth of the new state. Travelers from no other country wrote with more discernment about the young nation than the visitors from France. Leading them all in sharpness of observation and depth of understanding was Alexis de Tocqueville. His great work, *Democracy in America* (1835-1840), depicted the virtues and limitations of society in the United States. It both flattered and irritated Americans, but for Europeans it was *the* work on the New World. Its aristocratic author made plain to his fellows in the ruling classes of the Old World that democracy was the wave of the future and they had better learn to ride it or they would be swamped by it.

In the years of the Orleanist monarchy (1830-1848) French liberalism and radicalism reemerged from hibernation under the restored Bourbons. All kinds of plans for the renovation of society, ranging from utopian socialism to republicanism, were eagerly debated in this period. It was natural for those with a republican program to fix their eyes on America.

France Studies America's Constitution. No people studied the American constitution with deeper intensity than the French of this generation. Their interest was not that of the cloistered theorist; it was rather a matter of immediate concern for their future way of life. The events of 1848 and the establishment of the Second Republic fixed the attention of Frenchmen more firmly on the American example. At this moment, said a French newspaper in May 1848, "when France is in agitation, when thrones are falling, when all Europe is in rebellion,

and when old populations are preparing to adopt new
and better forms of government, it may be useful to
know the political and civil institutions which the republic
of the United States possesses."

Lucien Murat, a leader of the moment, declared: "Banished by the enemies of France I bring you from the
United States twenty-two years of experience and of republican opinions." The lesson drawn from America
which impressed Frenchmen most deeply was that "true
liberty was the daughter of order." Violence was the chief
danger to the security of the individual as well as to the
state. A moderate French newspaper in April 1848 expressed it simply: "One may without drenching oneself
with blood . . . be an excellent republican; there are
already more than fifty millions of that kind in the United
States." The republic inspired by Washington, said Lamar-
tine, "will triumph over the republic of Baboeuf, of Robespierre, and of Danton."

Tocqueville, a member of the Assembly chosen to draw
up a constitution for the Second Republic, had called attention to several elements in the American system which
had special appeal for him and for other Frenchmen
fearful of the emergence of a new absolutism. These New
World attractions were local self-government, an independent judiciary, and the federal system. Catholics
pointed to the rapid growth of their church in the United
States as proof of the wisdom of separating church and
state. In contrast to European countries which sought to
make the church an instrument of government, in America
she was entirely free and therefore flourishing.

Rival Views on America. Freedom of economic
enterprise and freedom of the press as practiced in the
United States were held up for French imitation. Opposition to following New World example rested on differing French traditions and ridicule of America's
pretensions to lead others to freedom when she mistreated
Indians and enslaved Negroes. In general it may be said
that America's example was quoted most ardently by
political moderates who were at the same time upholders
of a laissez-faire economy.

The constitution that finally emerged from the Assembly's debates showed no close adherence to American

precedent. American example did suggest the presidential office and the four-year term; apparently it was influential in fixing the basis of representation in the legislature. But the influence of American political ideas in France cannot be measured by clauses in a constitution. This constitution was soon to be made a mockery by Louis Napoleon, but American ideology and practice were to be a constant resource of hopeful Frenchmen. Where, they asked each other plaintively, is our George Washington?

Britain and the United States. Franco-American ties for the most part were ideological and the concern of a minority in each country. Only in periods of crisis in France was there relatively intense preoccupation by a large public with American relationships. On the other hand, Anglo-American relations were of continuous and deep concern to Britain and the United States. Large-scale emigration from the British Isles to the New World made the United States part of everyday consciousness to millions in the homeland. The closeness of economic ties in commerce and finance (each country was the other's best customer) further accented a mutual awareness. American deference to English literary preeminence (though sometimes reluctantly offered) was another link between the two communities. English conservatives and American republicans often found contact abrasive, but British radicals found it comforting and invigorating.

Anglo-American Rapprochement. The American Revolution, with its unresolved economic and boundary controversies, bequeathed a legacy that embittered Anglo-American relations for generations. And yet there were signs even on the morrow of America's independence that rapprochement could be achieved. In the 1780's German students of Anglo-American relations prophesied such rapprochement. Able diplomats in England and the United States strove with success toward the end of the eighteenth century to moderate the friction that heated tempers on both sides of the Atlantic. Maritime differences, conflicting territorial ambitions, irritations arising out of economic rivalry, American assertiveness, and British airy superiority all combined to divide the English-speaking peoples. But the striking fact is that apart from the War of 1812, differences were eventually composed.

Skeptical Britons and suspicious Americans found themselves practically yoked together as reluctant partners aiding the growth of the Atlantic Civilization. (*See Reading No. 16.*)

America "A Beacon of Freedom." Certain groups in England, from the days of the American Revolution, were devoid of skepticism in their idealization of the New World. For them there was little wrong in the American experiment and they constantly invoked its lessons in denouncing their own outmoded society. America had been a beacon to them in the eighteenth century; the light did not fail them in the nineteenth. The American Republic, said the radical London Working Men's Association in the 1830's, "is a beacon of freedom" for all mankind. Conservative *Blackwood's Magazine* testified regretfully to America's influence: "The current sets in strong and fast from the Transatlantic shores, and the old bulwarks of England are fast giving way before its fury."

Those who set their sights on this western beacon were, for the most part, workingmen and liberal members of the middle class. The latter were best represented by Richard Cobden and John Bright, known to the House of Commons as "the two members for the United States." As reformers looked across the Atlantic, the New World seemed to have much to teach the Old in reducing costs in litigation and in expanding the area of freedom in journalism, communications, education, religion, politics, land distribution, and business enterprise. As the *Westminster Review* observed, America had done most to fulfill the utilitarian principle of "the greatest happiness of the greatest number." Always, in England and on the continent, there was one reservation in the general chorus of liberal and radical praise of America—a lament for Negro slavery.

Conservatives Hostile to America. The attack on privilege, monarchy, the established church, and excessive costs of government gained weight during the debates on the Reform Bill of 1832. In the forefront of British consciousness, both conservative and radical, was the example of American experience. To conservatives the problem, as they saw it, was to withstand the "influence of the universal suffrage and republican government of the United States." Tyranny of the majority, thralldom for the minority were the alleged bitter fruits of democracy.

Chartists Applaud America.   Chartists, on the other hand, were nurtured on American principles, which, they believed, would one day triumph in their own country. Andrew Jackson was as much a hero to them as he was to many Americans. The National Union of the Working Classes, very active in behalf of suffrage reform, rarely omitted from a resolution or failed to hear from one of its speakers some reference to American economy in government. New World democratic refusal to tax itself for the support of privilege was strongly applauded. The Atlantic Republicans "have shown us that *men can eat,* and *drink,* and sleep, and have children and *homes,* and firesides, and *trade,* and *commerce,* and *agriculture,* and great moral and intellectual, as well as political weight in the world, and . . . encourage the arts and sciences . . . and yet have NO NATIONAL DEBT and NO KING."

When the House of Lords in October 1831 rejected the Reform Bill, the *Poor Man's Guardian* (circulating illegally in tens of thousands of copies) reminded its readers of the American Revolution, "the struggle for independence of an oppressed and despairing people." This great event constituted "the best precedent and guide to the oppressed and enslaved people of England in *their* struggle for the RIGHT OF REPRESENTATION FOR EVERY MAN."

Radicals Hail Americanization.   To the conservative cry of havoc to British institutions, radicals replied joyfully on the prospects of Americanizing their land. Americanized, they said, "means that the working classes should be made free citizens of the country enriched by their toil and defended by their courage. . . ." Through panic (1857) and Civil War democratic government seemed to give proof of strength superior to Old World monarchy, and the speed of American economic recovery on both occasions was impressive. America, her supporters boasted, was "the empire of the working man." No appeal to tradition, no authoritarian force in mid-nineteenth century could blot out the beacon of freedom that threw its rays into England.

THE SOCIAL CONSCIENCE OF THE ATLANTIC WORLD

In 1835, just before his life ended, James Madison told an English visitor that the United States had been "useful in proving things before held impossible." The young nation had shown that large-scale republican government was possible. It revealed also that a democratic society could enhance the status of women and could generate reforms to improve the spiritual breed of mankind in education, in penology, and through philanthropic institutions. Europeans expressed delighted astonishment at the many proofs of America's generous philanthropy, which they saw in United States hospitals, scientific institutions, colleges, and libraries.

Temperance Movement.   Americans were energetic in raising the unfortunate to the dignity of men. Their achievement was especially notable in the temperance movement which began in Philadelphia before the end of the eighteenth century. Benjamin Rush, who was most prominent in this cause, argued that intemperance was the parent of many social evils, including a corrupted civil society. A people befogged by strong drink, he said, "cannot long be a *free* people." Temperance societies under American initiative were formed on both sides of the Atlantic. Sweden's king spread American temperance propaganda through every parish of his kingdom. Ireland's Father Theobald Mathew became the most famous temperance advocate in the Atlantic world, traveling in the British Isles and America, winning many thousands to his side. To have gained commitment from large numbers of men to temperate drinking was a real social revolution and Europeans gratefully acknowledged the impetus that came from overseas.

Europe Studies American Penology.   The penitentiary system of the United States had been carefully studied by Europeans since the end of the eighteenth century. The penal system of Pennsylvania was especially admired overseas for its humanity and its apparent success in rehabilitating criminals. The Scandinavian countries adopted it, in modified form, and so did Belgium, Italy, and Prussia. Edward Livingston, a close student of England's Jeremy Bentham, published a revised penal code he had drawn up for Louisiana. It laid heavy emphasis on prevention rather than punishment of crime. Reformers throughout the Atlantic world acclaimed his imagination; the noted English authority, Sir Henry Maine, called him "the first legal genius of modern times."

Pacifism in the Atlantic Community. Dedicated men and women on both sides of the ocean sought, through beneficent punishment, to redeem the wayward. The task which the pacifist Elihu Burritt set himself was vaster, for he sought nothing less than the renunciation of war by all men. Peace societies had been formed in the United States and England soon after the War of 1812, and later on the continent. Burritt, a self-taught blacksmith learned in many fields, became an international courier to advance peace. He was largely responsible for the organization of international congresses which enlisted the support of such prominent personalities as Victor Hugo. Hugo himself looked for the eventual creation of the United States of Europe which, in association with the United States of America, would maintain the peace of the world.

Burritt, a skilled propagandist, placed monthly articles in forty important European newspapers which reached over a million readers. No American had ever had so large a European audience. More than any other person he was responsible for creating in Europe a mass sentiment favorable to peace. He identified his cause with the liberal program generally, believing that free trade among nations (an important liberal tenet) was one of the conditions for the maintenance of peace.

Feminism in America. Many of the crusaders for peace in mid-nineteenth century were women, and their participation in this enterprise was but one expression of the feminist movement in this period of Atlantic history.

American women, it had often been remarked by Europeans, were far freer in their social relations than women of the Old World. In the United States they preached to religious congregations, they were in the forefront of battles against slavery, inadequate education, backward treatment of the sick and insane. They met in national conventions, notably in 1848, to press for programs of social and political equality with men.

Feminism in Europe.   Their demand for the suffrage was echoed in England's *Westminster Review* (1851) by Mrs. John Stuart Mill. "Many of our readers will probably learn from these pages for the first time," she wrote, "that there has arisen in the United States . . . an organized agitation on a new question. . . . . This question is the enfranchisement of women; their admission, in law and in fact, to equality in all rights, political, civil, and social, with the male citizens of the community." She linked the struggle for the emancipation of women with the hopes of English and continental radicals, urging them to identify it with their demand for universal suffrage.

Women in other countries were likewise inspired by American example. Fredrika Bremer, the Swedish novelist, on her return from the United States devoted herself in the 1880's to the feminist cause. Progress in Sweden was painfully slow, but within a few years it did come in the assignment of women teachers in public schools, in partial control by women of their own wealth, and in a limited franchise for local offices. On both sides of the Atlantic the feminist movement was ridiculed, but its pioneers lived to have the last laugh. John Stuart Mill, in his famed *The Subjection of Women* (1869) threw his powerful influence to their side. He paid tribute to America's leadership; and his book, translated into many languages, gave irresistible momentum to this cause. But it is worth noting that Europe (in expanding higher education for women, for example) often waited upon American initiative.

Emma Willard, a pioneer feminist, successfully urged New York State to support a girl's seminary. She was a remarkable woman with a particular skill in composing textbooks for elementary schools. These books, in history, geography and other subjects, were sometimes translated and adopted in European schools. Miss Willard traveled to Europe, where she stirred up interest in education for women.

Education in the Atlantic Community.   On the elementary level influences in education in the Atlantic world moved both ways. Americans learned from Europeans the latest techniques in dealing with children of kindergarten age. Correspondents in the United States in the 1820's sent their ideas and books to Victor Cousin, the French master, who carefully preserved these signs of New World interest in his educational philosophy. Commissions were sent from the United States to Prussia, Switzerland, and other countries to investigate government support of public education. Americans were often impressed by what they saw, but in their own country they were insistent upon the secularization of the public school; it must be free of any sectarian influence they said. When Europeans debated the problem of support for public education, liberals and radicals among them argued for the American example. Englishmen and Frenchmen, from the 1830's on, constantly drew the attention of their respective countrymen to American practice, which, they said, avoided sectarian friction so common in Europe.

Democratization of Culture.   Throughout the North Atlantic Civilization determined efforts were made to further the democratization of culture. Often the initiative came from the Old World, as in the English Society for the Diffusion of Culture, or the mechanics' libraries of the British Isles. Quickly both of these were imitated in the United States, and soon the New World seemed to be outstripping the Old in its support of such agencies. Members of Parliament, when urging government funds for libraries, reminded opposing colleagues of American generosity in this matter. European observers always took note of the large per capita circulation of newspapers in America (far exceeding circulation in Britain, for example), a fact which helped explain for them the successful working of its democracy. The Old World was warned by its own educational leaders that it must follow American example in popularizing knowledge if it wished to avoid despotism and revolution. (*See Reading No. 17.*) Always in the minds of Jeffersonians, whether they lived

in America or in Europe, enlarging cultural opportunities
for the mass of men was a prime requirement for the
perpetuation of a democratic society.

American Deficiencies. On higher levels of learning
Americans were painfully conscious of their backward
state. William Ellery Channing in 1830 said his countrymen were generous in spreading elementary education
but, he complained, "we fall behind . . . in provision
for the liberal training of the intellect, for forming great
scholars. . . . There is among us much superficial knowledge, but little severe, persevering research; . . . little
resolute devotion to a high intellectual culture."

In the American environment of mid-nineteenth century
no theorist of the preeminent quality of the geologist Sir
Charles Lyell or Michael Faraday or Charles Darwin appeared. Tocqueville noted that Americans had not contributed much to basic science (he thought their spirit was
"averse to general ideas"). He remarked, however, that
they were quick to apply the findings of others to practical
ends.

Reform of Higher Education in America. Jefferson's cherished University of Virginia sought to strengthen
its staff by additions of European scholars. George Bancroft, before he became famous as historian, and George
Ticknor, while teaching Romance languages at Harvard,
struggled vainly in the attempt to reform the college
curriculum. Ticknor, who made a really distinguished contribution with his *History of Spanish Literature,* spent
much of his life in an effort to raise the standard of American scholarship. He, like Bancroft and a number of others
in the early years of the nineteenth century, had gone to
Göttingen, Germany, for graduate study.

Their experience opened their eyes to the inadequacies
of higher learning in America. "Every day I feel anew,"
wrote Ticknor (1815) "what a mortifying distance there
is between a European and an American scholar." With
prophetic insight he said that two or three generations
must pass away before scholarship in America would
reach European standards. In the years just before the
Civil War young Americans, among them Andrew D.
White and Daniel C. Gilman, returned from their European studies to embark on a lifelong enterprise of raising

academic standards in America. The first real success did not come, however, until the 1870's, with the founding of the Johns Hopkins University. (*See Reading No. 18.*)

German Culture in America. Bancroft and Ticknor were among the pioneers in introducing German culture in America. Even in earlier years, in the eighteenth century, a small number of Americans had been aware of the riches in German literature and scientific scholarship. But the real impact of the culture of Germany—her drama, her poetry and prose, her scholarship in theology, philology, and history, her traditions in the graphic arts—was not strongly felt until well into the nineteenth century.

Latin Heritage in America. In the generation after the War of 1812 Americans drew more frequently upon the cultural heritage of countries outside the British Isles. In addition to German culture, French civilization, which had long exercised its sway over many Americans, continued to fascinate. Certain features of it, not well known in America before, such as medical theory and practice, were now powerful enough to displace traditional British influences. Americans in increasing number began to find their way to Florence and Rome, to sit spellbound before artistic masterpieces which had been only names to them. So charmed were Americans by Italy that expatriate colonies were located there from pre-Civil War days. Spain, whose Cervantes was part of the literary inheritance of many Americans, had a powerful attraction for Ticknor, Longfellow, and the historian Prescott. It was a world filled with the wonder and romance of civilizations, Muslim and Catholic, alien to the Anglo-American Protestant inheritance in which they were bred.

The British Legacy. It was, however, the British inheritance which was dominant in American life. (*See Reading No. 19.*) It was traceable in the influence of her literature, her political philosophy (John Locke was still the leading political philosopher in America), her industrial and fine arts. The early nineteenth century in England's literary history was unsurpassed in splendor except for the Elizabethan flowering. A country which could produce a Coleridge, a Wordsworth, a Scott, a Burns, a Byron, a Shelley, a Keats, shone with especial brightness against the paler achievements of most other lands.

American Literature Abroad.   Basking in the light of this brilliance Sydney Smith in 1820 threw his derisive question at the United States, "Who reads an American book?" He had forgotten Franklin's popular acclaim and the Europeans' close study of Jonathan Edwards. In the main he was right, but only for the moment. Within a short time Washington Irving and James Fenimore Cooper were to have large audiences abroad. Other American names were soon added to theirs: William Ellery Channing, Longfellow, Emerson, Hawthorne, Melville, and the historians Bancroft and Prescott.

Poe had an especial appeal for the French, whose poets, among them Charles Baudelaire and Stéphane Mallarmé, were deeply influenced by him. Following the French lead, writers of prose and poetry in other countries gladly fell under the spell of Poe's style. The fame of Cooper, in particular, was an exchange from the New World for the overwhelming American popularity of Scott and, later, Dickens. It would seem that wherever the printed word could reach there was found a delighted reader of Cooper. As for Longfellow, he became in England as well as in America the most popular poet of his day. "No poet of our own or of any other land is so widely known," said the *London Times,* which added that he was the favorite of the educated as well as the masses.

Uncle Tom's Cabin.   A very special place in the literary annals of the Atlantic world was reserved for Harriet Beecher Stowe. Her *Uncle Tom's Cabin* was probably the most sensational success in publishing history. In England 1,500,000 copies were sold within a year of its first appearance. Numerous translations quickly followed picking up many more thousands of readers. Through the pathos of its dramatic story it won its place in readers' affections. The most effective propaganda ever written against slavery, its impact on Europe was to knit the widespread antislavery sentiment there with abolitionism in the United States.

Transatlantic Abolitionism.   Americans in northern states, and Europeans generally, lamented the existence of slavery. Americans (some of them Negroes) crossed to Europe to stir up public hostility to slavery and to raise funds for abolitionism. Europeans crossed to America to lend their oratorical skill and moral support to the same cause. Transatlantic cooperation in the movement against slavery was one of the most vigorous expressions of humanitarianism in the first half of the nineteenth century. (*See Reading No. 20.*)

Europe's Aristocracy Favors the South. *Uncle Tom's Cabin* helped win for the North a mass support in Europe on the outbreak of the Civil War. Europe's aristocrats, though disliking slavery, generally sided with the South. Fearing democracy, they wished for the defeat of the North and the disruption of the Union. The weight of the United States would then be much less in world affairs. The division of the country into two or more sovereignties would make the former United States a prey to the intrigues of great powers who could then play off the various parts of the former Union against each other.

Europe's Democrats Favor the North. Sentiment among middle-class liberals and workingmen usually sided with the North, for its cause was identified with that of political, social, and economic freedom as well as physical freedom. (*See Reading No. 21.*) The hopes of democratic republicans in Europe sank when Northern troops faltered; they rose on the winged words of Lincoln and the success of Northern arms.

When stillness settled over Appomattox, the future of democracy seemed secure. The American minister at Brussels, H. S. Sanford, had been told that Northern victory would have "a profound and far-reaching influence in the world; that from it would date a new era of progress and reform in Europe." Northern defeat on the other hand would "cause a reaction from the present liberal tendencies of the age." Berlin workingmen cheered the North, while British workingmen were emboldened to press forward with their demand for suffrage. Charles Francis Adams, American minister to London, reported in 1865 that the "extraordinary deference formerly paid to mere rank without regard to personal qualities, is much worn away." He looked "for decided progress in enlarging the popular features of the constitution" and the diminution of aristocratic influence. British workingmen won the vote in 1867.

Lincoln and Europe.   The rejoicing of the many in

Europe for the end of the war in America was suddenly transformed into grief when Lincoln died. All Europe paid homage to his grandeur. The demonstrations, said a French publication, showed how "popular the ideas of liberty and equality have become, as they are represented by the United States. Over the ashes of the President of the American Republic the whole of Europe has come to confess her democratic faith."

— 8 —

EMIGRATION AND THE ATLANTIC ECONOMY IN THE 19TH CENTURY

America was for millions of prospective European emigrants a living example of a superior way of life. To the scornful charge that they were building castles in the air, emigrants responded with quiet stubbornness: No, they had the address, on the ground, in Pennsylvania or Ohio or Michigan, across the Atlantic. Many emigrants were mistaken, for their castles never did materialize, but they were prepared to make great sacrifices to win a habitable home.

Emigration Spurs Democracy. Emigration, or the threat of emigration, was a weapon in an earlier arsenal of democracy. The Revolution in America had helped defeat reaction in England in the 1780's, and half a century later the existence of cheap lands in the West probably moderated the reaction that followed the Napoleonic wars. Village Englishmen were shaken from their dull apathy and sullen discontent by news from the American West.

A farmer who had emigrated to the United States wrote a glowing account of his new home in Iowa. His letter, said a contemporary, "was read at the village inn and at the Methodist Chapel every Sunday until it was nearly worn out. The Lord had now opened a door of escape." Having made up their minds to leave, "the whole village was at work in packing and mending clothes. A farewell service was held in the Methodist Chapel, which was crowded, and the service lasted through night till daybreak." Then in the glorious springtime, some thirty-three men, women, and children marched through the village singing hymns. The whole village turned out, and many accompanied them for miles. "Good-bye, God bless you! rang from every cottage door." Prayers were said for the exiles until news arrived of their safe arrival in their American home. "This induced others, in batches of threes and fours, to follow for several years."

Reaction to Emigration in Scandinavia. And so the emigrant stream grew from 10,000 annually in the 1820's to some 300,000 in the 1850's. "America letters," "America books," and oral reports of returned travelers made the seemingly remote lands of the western Atlantic an intimate part of native European consciousness. Reformers in Scandinavia openly stated that they used the question of emigration as a "vehicle for social legislation." One Swedish writer noted that, "To discuss Swedish emigration is the same as to discuss 'Sweden'; there is hardly a single political, social or economic problem in our country, which has not been conditioned, directly or indirectly, by the phenomenon of emigration."

In Norway, emigration stimulated discussions for reform of her agriculture; mechanization and modernization were urged upon her farmers. Leaders of workingmen like Marcus Thrane in Norway urged large-scale emigration to compel the upper classes to realize the value of labor. Emigration also focused attention upon demands for complete religious freedom in Scandinavia. (*See Reading No. 22.*)

Emigration Chiefly to America. From all of Europe, first from its northern and western reaches, then from its eastern and southern regions, went the millions to till America's soil, to work in its mines and factories, to build its arteries of communications—canals and railroads. The mass migration from Europe in the century after the Napoleonic wars was one of the greatest movements of people in all history. While Latin America absorbed several millions (Italians and Germans especially) and Canada took over 3,000,000 from the British Isles alone, the United States was the objective of most emigrants. The great majority of emigrant Irishmen settled here; so did nine-tenths of departing Germans. (*See Reading No. 23.*) Of the Swedish migrants, 98% went to the United States, where they were joined by 96% of Norway's emigrants.

Over 39,000,000 (including some 5,000,000 from countries in the Western Hemisphere) entered the United States from 1820 (when records began to be kept) until mid-twentieth century. This host brought with them their arts and crafts and small sums of capital. When totaled, the capital was a respectable addition to America's liquid assets, especially in pre-Civil War United States. Not all those who left for America became permanent residents of the New World. It has been estimated that about one-third returned to their original homelands.

Factors in Migration.   Emigration was heaviest in periods of American prosperity and European economic crisis. Agricultural disaster (failure of potato crops, diminishing farm income—due sometimes to cheaper American imports) and dislocation brought on by a shift from handicrafts to the factory system help to explain the exodus from Europe. The volume of emigration was also related to the rate of capital investment in the old country. Heavy investment provided more job opportunities at home; a decline in local capital outlay diminished economic activity and spurred emigration. Three periods—1847-1854, 1880-1890, 1909-1914—were years of most intense emigration. In a span of twenty-five years, over seventeen millions of hopeful, sometimes frightened people crossed the sea.

Most emigrants came from inland regions where they knew only placid waters. The ocean seemed a mysterious and dangerous unknown. The voyage west in a sailing vessel was usually tedious, quarters were cramped, and mortality heavy (particularly among the undernourished

Irish) when disease broke out. Fares from England in the 1830's were £5 or less. Canadian lumber vessels, returning from the British Isles, carried Irishmen to Quebec for £2 10s. For $5 an Irishman could get to Newfoundland by sleeping on the deck of a fishing boat and eating salt cod. Most of these Irish emigrants did not linger long in Canada. Jobs were more plentiful in the United States and land there was easier to acquire.

All peoples had their emigrant songs—poems of tearful farewell and expressions of hope for the good life in a new land. The "Lament of the Irish Emigrant" spoke of a land where

> They say there's bread and work for all,
> And the sun shines always there.

A Norwegian poet, though sentimental, remembered reality;

> Farewell, Norway, and God bless thee;
> Stern and severe wert thou always, but as
> A mother I honor thee, though thou
> Skimped my bread.

Emigrant Ambitions. Freight wagons trucking American cotton southward from Le Havre returned from Basel and Strasbourg with gaily clad emigrants for ships bound for New Orleans. In time Bremen and Hamburg succeeded to the coveted position held by Le Havre in the lucrative emigrant trade. From New Orleans these newcomers spread up the Mississippi Valley. Most immigrants, however, found their way into the New World by way of the port of New York. Edwin Bottomley was one of them. He left England in 1842 to prevent his children from falling into the pattern of their elders, going into the mill as factory workers. Bottomley went to Wisconsin, acquired eighty acres at $1.25 an acre, and after hard but gratifying work, insured the future he desired for his family. "Thank God," he wrote, "I have not to rouse my children at the sound of a bell from their beds and Drag them through the pelting storm of a Dark winters morning to earn a small pitance at a factory."

Emigrant Remittances. Though many emigrants left for America on their own resources, others were assisted by remittances forwarded by friends and relatives who had preceded them. By 1863 the Irish had sent home twenty million pounds, thus paying most of the expenses of emigration with money earned in America. When one remembers that these immigrants had low-paid jobs in their new homes, this sum represents a remarkable example of self-denial and loyalty to those still in Ireland.

Emigrant peoples as a whole were very generous in remittances to former homelands. It has been estimated that from 25% to 70% of the immigrants to the United States were provided with transportation funds from America. In the early years of the twentieth century the foreign-born in the United States were sending overseas $250,000,000 annually. In one village in Sweden, remittances from America averaged $5 per person; this apparently small sum equaled about 15% of the annual income of a hired man. The total remitted to Sweden in the 1920's was equal to the sum spent by the government on old age pensions. (*See Reading No. 24.*) A Norwegian has estimated that his emigrant countrymen during a period of one hundred years sent back home about $600,000,000. Some of it went for passage money, but there was much left for farm equipment, new clothes, books, and medical service.

Impact of Dollars on Europe. All European countries with sizable emigrant groups in the United States felt the impact of American dollars. This welcome flow of currency helped relieve poverty in many communities and furnished capital to pay off mortgages and improve farmers' holdings. It helped reduce the rate of interest at home and put local currency, as in Greece and Italy, on a sounder basis. Sometimes the cost of living rose because of the influx of American dollars.

Effects of Emigration upon Europe. During years of increased migration, "America auctions" of peasant lands glutted the real estate market. It was then that landless agrarians could buy at low prices. Repatriated emigrants frequently invested their savings, accumulated in America, in homesteads in the Old Country. In one Swedish district (1907) with over two thousand farms, one in six was owned by Swedish-Americans. In another community in Sweden more than one-fourth of the farm owners had lived in America.

Release of the pressure of excess population by emigration helped stem the "proletarianization" of rural society in many parts of Europe. The departure of large numbers from such countries as Ireland and Italy caused an increase in the wage rates of those remaining. Large landowners living in regions of heavy emigration were spurred to introduce machinery. The balance of the sexes was upset, since it was the young males who were usually in the majority on emigrant ships. Emigration of youth diminished the birth rate at home and left a disproportionate number of older people in the Old World.

The return tide brought back to Europe people with changed ideas as well as changed fortunes. The successful repatriate often built a better home than the one he had left as an emigrant; it was his habit to display his superior wealth. In a number of Italian communities whole quarters were inhabited by the "Americani." (*See Reading No. 25.*) Generally speaking, successful returned emigrants had a higher standard of living than those who had stayed at home. In Norway they were said to work faster and show more initiative. Retired repatriates were conscious of having earned their ease. "One thing I will always remember about America," said one, "was that I gave it the most productive years of my life."

Italians, like their fellow repatriates in northern Europe, could not conceal their contempt for old-fashioned ways of doing things and for the ancient differences that set off class from class. America's economic strength, her political example, and her moral influence made her a powerful force in dissolving the remains of feudal society in Europe. Together the Old World and the New established more firmly the democratic tradition in the lands bordering the North Atlantic.

THE ATLANTIC ECONOMY

Commerce of the Atlantic World.   The whole Atlantic economy was profoundly affected by this surge of millions of people to and from the continent of North America. Leading ports of emigrant embarkation—Hamburg, Bremen, Liverpool, Naples, and Genoa—were heavily dependent upon this trade for their prosperity. New York, as the chief port of debarkation and the main channel for incoming and outgoing freight, rose to leadership in the North Atlantic economy.

For a long time, however, London's role was preeminent as the financial center of the Atlantic world. The House of Baring through most of the nineteenth century supplied the financial requirements for much of American enterprise. Construction of American communications, canals, and railroads was made possible by European financial aid. Commercial ties were especially close between Britain and the United States in the forty years before the Civil War. In that period nearly half of American exports went to Britain, which in turn supplied 40% of United States imports.

British Contributions to American Economy. New techniques in American industry owed much to European example. English, Scottish, and Welsh workers, in particular, carried with them their skills learned in the most advanced industrial community of the nineteenth century. They transferred these skills directly to mines and factories overseas. Most of England's silk industry, ruined by French competition, migrated to Paterson, New Jersey, after the Civil War. Nearly every collier in South Wales in the middle of the nineteenth century had a relative or close friend in America and was himself thinking of leaving. Most of the important advances in manufacture of rails, steel, and wrought-iron down to 1880 originated in Britain and were transferred to the United States. But by 1890 American steel mills had surpassed British inventiveness and productive capacity.

British immigrants were especially influential in the development of American labor unions, bringing to them much of the spirit of their Old World trade-unionism. But many who had arrived in America as workers, finding that climbing the social ladder was easier than in Britain, became foremen, superintendents, and even company owners. After 1900 the British were usually supplanted in American mills and mines by newer immigrants from eastern and southern Europe.

Contributions by Other Europeans. Pottery and chinaware production in Pennsylvania owed much to earlier German immigrants. Another wave of German immigrants after 1848 included skilled craftsmen who brought to America their specialized knowledge in book-binding, lithography, printing, brewing, and the making of fine pianos. Transplanted French and Swiss built up America's watchmaking industry. Italians brightened the musical life of America and took an important part, too, in developing her wine industry.

America Speeds Up Communications. While the United States was heavily indebted to European capital, technology, and immigrant labor for its remarkably rapid economic growth, its reciprocal contribution to Europe's economy was of a high order. In exchange for the British-invented railroad, Americans gave to Europe urban street-car lines. Americans were especially imaginative in speeding up comunications of all kinds. Samuel F. B. Morse did it with the telegraph; Captain Matthew F. Maury (1847) did it with his publication *Wind and Current Chart of the North Atlantic,* which indicated the fastest routes across the ocean; Cyrus W. Field did it with the Atlantic cable.

Europeans, deeply impressed by America's advanced river steamboats, which could transport heavy loads in shallow, treacherous rivers, copied them. Edward Church (1779-1845), a far-wandering Bostonian, was largely responsible for the promotion of satisfactory steamboat navigation in several countries of western Europe in the 1820's. François-Prudent Bourdon (1797-1865), who had eagerly studied American craft in their native waters, returned to France in the 1830's to become her most ingenious designer. His boats, including those nostalgically named *Mississippi* and *Missouri,* conquered the river Rhône. A journey from Arles to Lyons, which once took thirty-five days by land freight, was now covered in less than thirty hours.

Mass Production in the Atlantic Community. America's contribution to the development of mass production was readily acknowledged in the nineteenth century. Eli Whitney's adoption of the principle of inter-changeable parts in the manufacture of firearms success-fully established standardization. Samuel Colt, of revolver fame, carried the system to England, which became con-vinced of his superior achievement (in price and quality) in arms manufacture. From the 1850's on, the principle of standardization gradually won its way in Europe. American tools and machines were being exported to Europe; and mass-produced goods (such as factory-made shoes) were eliminating handicraftsmen.

American Machinery and Products in Europe. Colt had displayed his revolver at the first World's Fair in London in 1851. It was this fair which really opened Europe's eyes to American technological accomplishments. The London *Times,* ordinarily not kindly to America, said that performances at the fair revealed that every practical success belonged to transatlantic exhibitors. "Their reaping machine has carried conviction to the heart of the British agriculturist. Their revolvers threaten to revolutionize military tactics . . . Their yacht [*America*] takes a class to itself." Cyrus H. McCormick's reaper and mower proved themselves superior to all competitors. From then on American agricultural machines were adopted in Europe, where, as in the United States, they transformed farming. These machines, by displacing man power, accelerated far-reaching economic and social changes in Europe, promoting urbanization and further emigration.

It was not only machinery from America which affected the way of life in Europe. It was her agricultural products themselves. The role of the potato in Europe is a familiar story, and so too are the tragic consequences of crop failure in countries like Ireland with a "potato standard" diet. A leading authority on this subject, R. N. Salaman, says that seemingly prosperous England was in grave danger of falling to a "potato standard" and was only saved "by larger supplies of cheap food from America."

Impact of American Agriculture on Europe. The cost of transporting a bushel of wheat from Chicago to England dropped in the second half of the nineteenth century from 37¢ to 10¢. Western Europe's grain growers could not meet American competition, and many communities shifted over to raising cattle. English agriculture suffered disaster. Acreage sown to wheat there fell off by 40% between 1869 and 1887, but overseas imports cut the price of wheat in England almost in half. Though American farm wages were four times the average in Prussia, the latter's cost for producing a bushel of wheat was 80¢, against 40¢ in the western United States. Denmark by importing cheap American feed grains made cattle raising and dairy production profitable enterprises.

American pork was also underselling homegrown pork in Europe. To combat this competition from the United States most European countries adopted high-tariff policies to limit American agricultural imports. Bismarck in order to exclude New World pork charged that American hogs were infected with trichinosis. At the same time he gave a clean bill of health to German hogs. Despite such action American agriculture, more and more mechanized, continued to expand its output and contribute greatly to Europe's diet.

In addition to foodstuffs, other products of American soil—cotton and tobacco—were fundamental to the growth of the Atlantic economy. Tobacco had been important from the seventeenth century, but now European governments sought to monopolize its sale and make the profits a regular part of the nation's income. Taxes on tobacco became an important item in national budgets.

Europe's Dependence on American Cotton. Eli Whitney's cotton gin by making the cultivation of cotton profitable fastened Negro slavery on the United States. But it also was responsible for speeding up the growth of the textile industry in the whole Atlantic community. The mills of England and France counted heavily upon America's cotton. In the years before the Civil War, England drew 85% of her raw cotton from America's Deep South. France, too, after the Napoleonic wars found the United States her chief supplier of cotton. In the generation following 1815 French industrial workers began to be far better clothed, for cotton clothing became common and cheap, much cheaper than linen.

Raw cotton was the largest item in United States exports for many years. In the first half of the nineteenth century, especially, this agricultural export paid for much of America's imports of manufactured goods. It almost seemed as if the whole Atlantic economy was so intimately bound up with cotton that it justified the proud title "King." It is clear, however, that its majesty was exaggerated. In English eyes wheat competed in importance with cotton. Also California gold, after 1851 to the end of the Civil War, helped in balancing America's books in international trade.

Shift of Economic Leadership to America. Despite the great growth of the economy of the United States, the nation still had an unfavorable balance of trade which was made good by continued loans from Europe. Capital invested in America had for many years received double the return available to it in England. In the years 1881-1885 economic relationships in the Atlantic community underwent marked changes. The United States now outranked the United Kingdom as the greatest center of manufacturing output. Thereafter America's lead increased rapidly, so that by the turn of the century the balance of economic power in the Atlantic world had shifted decisively in her favor. At that time her productive capacity exceeded that of Great Britain and Germany combined.

Interdependence of Atlantic Community. The twentieth century is more conscious than was the nineteenth of the fact that the Atlantic community should be thought of as one economy. Its economic interdependence was obvious long ago. European and American business cycles coincided fairly closely. Labor, capital, and commodities all moved within the Atlantic community as they did within a single nation's boundaries. Some perceptive individuals, including Brooks Adams and Sir Robert Giffen, saw it all clearly. Giffen remarked, "Now the idea of a new Europe on the other side of the Atlantic affects every speculation, however much the new people keep themselves aloof from European politics. European governments can no longer have the notion that they are playing the first part on the stage of the world's political history. And this sense of being dwarfed will probably increase in time." The growth of nationalism in the nineteenth century, however, obscured for the many the links attaching the various parts of the Atlantic community to one another. In the twentieth century came a deeper realization of its unique qualities.

— 9 —

TOWARD MATURITY IN THE 20TH CENTURY

Throughout the Atlantic community more and more people were gradually becoming aware of the economic interdependence of its various members. In the cultural relations between the Old and New Worlds an important change occurred also. The New World, on higher levels of intellectual and artistic activity, had been for a long time heavily indebted to Europe. While American contributions (in literature, for example) were often on a par with those of Europe, the balance on the whole was strongly in the Old World's favor. Since the last decades of the nineteenth century the standard of achievement has become more nearly equal on the two sides of the Atlantic; America attained growing importance as a prominent new center of world culture. The increased number of Nobel prizes awarded to Americans in recent years attests to this fulfillment of promise.

Recognition of Political Interdependence Lags. The economic and cultural maturity so manifest in the North Atlantic community was, however, not matched by a commensurate political maturity. Old barriers that were leaped or bypassed in trade, finance, education, science, literature, art, proved formidable obstacles to international political organization. The modern world has offered the paradox of economic and cultural cosmopolitanism living side by side with a parochial political mind.

The economic power of the North Atlantic community was vastly increased in the years after the 1880's. German productivity caught up with and surpassed Britain's. The familiar indices of strength—coal production, steel tonnage, ship construction, energy output, transportation facilities—all showed great gains in countries of the

91

Western World. To the established centers of economic power was added another in this period—Canada.

Canada Adds Economic Weight to the Atlantic Community. Although Canada's population is that of a small country (about fifteen million by mid-twentieth century) she has long been able to make a significant contribution to world economy through her agricultural exports, and more recently by her manufacturing and mining capacity. Because of her standard of living, one of the highest in the world, she and the United States consume a volume of goods wholly out of proportion to their population numbers. The North Atlantic community as a whole comprises about one-sixth of the world's population, but its productive power and consumption of the earth's resources greatly exceed that proportion.

Canadian-American Cross Migration. The economic interrelationship of the Old World and the New became, in time, more complex. Canadians crossed over the border by the tens of thousands to work in New England mills or take up land in the western states of the Union. In 1930 three and a third million people born of Canadian parents were living in the United States. One-quarter of Canada's population left their native land to find in the United States a safety valve for unfulfilled ambitions at home. (*See Reading No. 26.*)

The trek was reversed when farmers and prospectors from the United States sought their fortunes to the north, in Canada. In 1931 almost 350,000 American-born were living there. The investments of Americans in Canadian enterprise eventually reached such large dimensions as to justify speaking of these two countries as members almost of a single economy.

Inter-American Labor Migration. North American capital vied with European capital in developing the resources of Latin America, too, and ultimately claimed the larger share. While Mexico drew on United States capital for the expansion of her economy, the United States drew on her southern neighbor for a much-needed supply of labor to work on the farms and in the towns of the Southwest. When in the 1920's the United States drastically cut down the numbers of European immigrants to be admitted, a changed pattern of labor movement resulted. Vastly increased numbers of Mexicans, Puerto Ricans, and residents of other West Indian islands moved (temporarily or permanently) into the United States. Within the United States itself a striking rearrangement of the working force was brought about, in part at least by cutting off the traditional European supply of labor. Millions of Negroes moved out of the South into northern towns and cities to fill the void left by curtailment of immigration from Europe.

America the World's Financial Center. Down to 1914 America was still debtor to Europe, to the estimated sum of over four billion dollars. But some years earlier the New World's finances had already grown strong enough to be called on to render aid to Britain. This was striking evidence of an altered relationship in the Atlantic community. This change, early apparent to such able students as Brooks Adams, became clear enough for all to see by the close of World War I. The drain on Europe's resources was so great that former creditors became borrowers, and the United States emerged as the world's strongest financial center. American economic power was also dramatically revealed in the ability to dispatch and sustain a vast army in Europe. Her financial power was displayed in the billions of dollars loaned to her allies.

The economic interconnection between countries on the two sides of the Atlantic was evident in peace as in war. The relatively small investments of American capital in Europe before 1900 swelled to imposing proportions, more than five billions by 1930. Large enterprises in America—Ford, General Motors, General Electric, Westinghouse, the American Express Company among others —established branches overseas or bought into related businesses. The flow of European capital to America took on more of a speculative cast with the desire to share in the boom stock-market of the 1920's. Modern means of communication make it possible to move liquid capital from place to place rapidly, so that it is sometimes hard to say to which community it really belongs.

America Attains Cultural Maturity. The rise of the New World to eminence in the arts and sciences came more slowly than in commerce and industry. First-rate minds in America in the nineteenth century too often lived isolated from one another and thus could not exert the impact that an associated intellectual leadership in Europe was able to offer. In time, frequently with European example as guide, remarkable advances were made in the United States. Most notable improvement came in the universities.

With the establishment of Johns Hopkins in 1876, Americans for the first time had a real university. They had been aiming for it for years; and when it happened, progress in the whole university world was rapid. Inspiration had come from Europe, mainly Germany, whose schools transatlantic scholars had been attending for decades. In the century following the time when several New Englanders (Ticknor and Bancroft among them) took their degrees at Göttingen, some ten thousand Americans entered German universities. Not all of them were serious students, but those who were, including the historian John Lothrop Motley, brought back with them a standard of achievement higher than that in the United States. Ticknor had once complained that Americans did not really know the meaning of scholarship. But once they understood it their revitalized universities trained large numbers of young men and women to become distinguished philologists, historians, economists, and scientists.

European-American Cultural Relations. Americans have always followed avidly the latest creations of European genius. Darwin captured men's minds on both sides of the Atlantic, though he had his detractors in America as at home. Most of the great names in medicine—Lister, Pasteur, Virchow—and in science—Maxwell, Hertz, Rutherford, Curie, Einstein—were European. But even in the nineteenth century, American contributions to the first rank were not negligible. Lewis Henry Morgan, the anthropologist, was readily acknowledged by his contemporaries as a truly original mind. His studies of ancient society, based on close observation of the American Indian, had a profound influence on anthropologists everywhere.

In the post-Civil War generation, America's most distinguished name in science was that of Josiah Willard Gibbs, Yale professor of mathematical physics. Recognition came slowly; Europeans were the first to discern his genius, which lay in the field of thermodynamics. Gibbs was mainly responsible for founding a new science, physical chemistry. Until well into the twentieth century, however, Europeans generally led the way in framing the theories which opened new paths of research. Americans were quick to see the direction these paths took, and while they too appreciated "pure" research, the strong accent on business in their civilization directed special attention to technology.

European writers and artists found fault with the stress on business in their own society, but they had less to complain of than their American contemporaries. It was probably easier for an artist to survive in Europe than in America. At any rate Americans thought so. (*See Reading No. 27.*) As expatriates they certainly found Europe more congenial to their temper and way of life than their native land, although it was the latter that usually patronized them. France and Italy were their destinations, and they dutifully sat disciple-like before dead and living masters. A few became masters themselves, notably Whistler and Sargent.

Architecture in the Atlantic Community. It was in architecture rather than in painting that Americans excelled. Louis Sullivan and more particularly his pupil Frank Lloyd Wright captured the imagination of architects everywhere. Traditional structures gave way under their hands to original designs identifying their creations with the local terrain and the temper of the times. American architects created the skyscraper, whose daring thrust has dazzled countless visitors on their entry to New York's harbor.

On the other hand, in designs for community living Europeans won admiring comment from overseas. The Swiss-French Le Corbusier attracted attention by his great originality; Walter Gropins and his colleages in the German Bauhaus were an inspiration to many Americans; while the English example in town planning was thought to be superior to American accomplishment.

European-American Literary Relations. Europe's masters in literature had a devoted following overseas. The transatlantic audience for Shaw, Wells, Galsworthy, and Joyce, as well as authors of a later generation, was possibly larger than in Britain. Continental writers, especially the French Marcel Proust and André Gide and the German Thomas Mann, won both critical and popular recognition in America. (*See Reading No. 28.*)

In a reverse view, people had long stopped asking, "Who reads an American book?" Apparently many Europeans did, to judge by their familiarity with Henry James, William Dean Howells, Jack London, Mark Twain, and especially Walt Whitman. For the European, Whitman has been the poet of democracy, an explosive force in liberating men's minds. Upton Sinclair and Sinclair Lewis had a large popular audience abroad. In after years the transcendent influence of Ernest Hemingway and William Faulkner made for a kind of American literary *imperium,* young European writers acting as willing "colonials." The export of Eugene O'Neill's dramas and the musical plays of his countrymen has canceled much of America's indebtedness to the European stage.

In earlier years Emerson had left a deep impress on Europe's imagination. As John Morley put it, he was "one of the wise masters who breathed into other men a strong desire after the right governance of the soul." Emerson won heartfelt respect as the "philosopher of democracy." At a later time when Europeans thought of American philosophy, the name of William James was always foremost; pragmatism was America's special contribution. John Dewey's name was better known among Europeans than James's, particularly his views on progressive education. His book *Democracy and Education* became a guide to educators everywhere.

The Americanization of the World. It was on a level less exalted than that of the philosophers that America made its strongest impact in the Atlantic Civilization. When William T. Stead, the English journalist, published his *The Americanization of the World* in 1901, he maintained that many countries were being transformed by American economic patterns, products, machines, journalism, educational practices, and religious ideals. American evangelists—Dwight L. Moody and Ira D. Sankey, the hymn singer—stirred the religious emotions of more Britons than any of her native preachers. (*See Reading No. 29.*)

Although England's contribution to the democratization

of culture in the Atlantic community has been substantial over the past three centuries, the United States in the twentieth century has surpassed her. (*See Reading No. 30.*) American newspapers, books, magazines, radio, television, movies, popular music (notably jazz), have been potent influences on the mass mind everywhere. The American ideal of education for all has been provocative. British "educationists" in particular, though recognizing certain deficiencies in American schooling, have been impressed by the venturesome quality of academic life in the United States.

America Raises Standard of Living for Masses. While it is true that all members of the Atlantic community, in uneven degree, have shared in the creation of a democratic culture, it must be admitted that in meeting the economic requirements of a democratic society the American contribution has been unique. Americans, said W. E. Rappard (*The Secret of American Prosperity,* p. 16) produced the most wealth "not so much because their territory had been richly provided with natural resources, as because they have succeeded in making much better use of human labor, in their own country and abroad, than have any of their rivals in the rest of the world."

The United States saw the full effects of the discovery that mass production was not of much use without mass consumption. The latter could be achieved by stimulating demand through high-pressure salesmanship and by mass distribution. To bolster mass distribution, credit (once restricted to a few, presumably good risks) was now vastly extended to embrace almost everybody with almost any desire. Thus a high standard of living was created even for the majority of workingmen. The wealthy of Europe as well as many of their intellectuals often disparaged America's standard of living, pointing to its materialistic aspects. No doubt all that glittered was not gold, but it was hard to dissuade Europe's masses from wishing for some of America's glitter. For the most part Europe's middle class and workingmen were unimpressed by hostile criticism of America's materialism. Rather they were impressed by the fact that a way of living once thought possible only for the few had been created for the many. (*See Reading No. 31.*)

Transatlantic Cooperation in Social Programs.

Here then is one of the great, relatively quiet revolutions
in history. For the mass of men the area of freedom—political, economic, cultural—has been immensely enlarged
in less than a century in the North Atlantic community.
It has been a cooperative effort. Utopian dreamers in
Europe stirred American disciples to consider ways of
reorganizing society. In a reverse impact, the American
Henry George was credited by a noted British authority
at the end of the nineteenth century with having "exercised a more directly powerful formative and educational
influence over English radicalism of the last fifteen years
than any other man." German initiative in establishing
social insurance ultimately led to the adoption of similar
legislation elsewhere in the Atlantic community. Ideas to
better society were hurried to and fro across the Atlantic,
and their practical realization was the work of many
hands.

Criticism of America by Europe's "Left." A dis-
quieting aspect in the later evolution of the North Atlantic
community has been the loss of confidence in the United
States by many European workers and intellectuals. Once
it was the upper classes of the Old World who distrusted
the New World while the proletariat and intellectuals
sung its praises. But the latter, by the end of the nineteenth
century, in large numbers turned to Karl Marx instead of
Jefferson for guidance. The heritage of free political institutions in most countries of northern and western
Europe, however, proved enduringly strong. The rise of
totalitarianism in the years after World War I shocked
members of the Atlantic community into more vivid realization of a common devotion to their heritage.

Though the Western World had achieved a high degree
of cosmopolitanism, it was politically fragmented. The
barriers erected by nationalism were less yielding than
those erected by religion or economics. But these formidable obstacles to international cooperation gradually gave
way before the threatened collapse of the whole structure
of western civilization in the twentieth century.

Woodrow Wilson and International Order. The
age-old dream of an international organization of states
to enforce peace refused to die. Halting steps toward it
were taken at the turn of the twentieth century with arbi-

tration treaties and the Hague conferences on disarmament. Rivalries of the great powers made a shambles of these pacific movements in 1914. Out of the war was born a stronger realization of the need to substitute international order for international anarchy. Leadership came from several lands, but one of the most vigorous voices was that of the American President, Woodrow Wilson. For a glorious moment in 1918 he was hailed by a fervent Europe as a new Messiah.

More clearly than most of his countrymen, Wilson saw that America's traditional political isolationism was outmoded in the modern world. Suddenly, or so it seemed, the greatness of America's power was revealed, and whatever she did or did not do with it was to profoundly affect peoples everywhere. Wilson sought to convince fellow Americans that great-power status demanded great-power action. The action then required was the formation of the League of Nations and the winning of adherence to it. Success almost crowned his efforts, but mistakes in his tactics and misrepresentation by his opponents snatched defeat out of seeming victory. Had United States membership in the League been then secured it would have constituted a fundamental reorientation in the American outlook on foreign affairs.

As it was, the score of years following Wilson's temporary failure was a period when Americans had to exercise great-power responsibilities, even though their posture was one of reluctance. The mood of the country seemed to be expressed in legislation in the 1930's designed to insure the comfort of neutrality should war come again. Nazi totalitarianism and Japanese imperialism destroyed the illusory shield Americans had so wistfully constructed.

The United Nations. This time American opinion decisively shifted to willing acceptance of membership in the United Nations. President Franklin D. Roosevelt had carefully prepared Americans for this reversal in their historic foreign policy, and the rout of isolationist elements seemed complete. Victory over fascism in 1945 coincided with mutual congratulations among the victors that international anarchy would thenceforth be curbed by the power of the United Nations.

American Leadership Against Communist Imperi-

alism. Nationalism, however, was not dead. Indeed in Africa and Asia it was given explosive impetus by World War II. But more threatening was the enhanced power of another totalitarianism—Soviet communism. Into the vacuum left by German and Japanese collapse sped Russian troops, agents, and subversive forces of every variety. It almost seemed as if this global war had been fought to make the world safe for communism. Bold, imaginative policies, the Marshall Plan, the Truman Doctrine, were devised to bolster sagging economies and defenses in western and southern Europe and render them less susceptible to communist infiltration. These programs strengthened democratic elements in Europe and almost certainly prevented some nations from being lost to the world of democracy. The economic recovery of the Atlantic community so soon after an exhausting struggle was an amazing achievement, another revelation of America's power and Europe's indomitable will.

Economic rehabilitation for the eastern half of the North Atlantic community was supplemented by a plan for military defense of this area against continued pressure from Russia. That defense appeared in the North Atlantic Treaty Organization (NATO) which by elastic geographical interpretation embraced Mediterranean powers as well. Though NATO was conceived as a deterrent against possible Russian aggression, the forces available to it were not adequate to the task of withstanding for long a massive attack. As time went on, American military strategy seemed to rest more and more on atomic weapons to counterbalance communism's superiority in man power. But American fire power in atomic weapons was also challenged by Russian possession of nuclear bombs. Thus each country's nuclear strength canceled out the other's, leaving, however, Russia with great superiority in "old-fashioned" military strength.

Decline of Europe.   Two world wars left two superpowers, the United States and Russia, to dominate the globe. Nations which had once been great powers in their own right, England and France particularly, had to make a tremendous psychological adjustment to their grievous change in fortunes. The erosion of European empires in Asia and Africa accented the declining weight of Europe in the world. Historians began to speak of the passing of the European Age.

Potential Strength of United Europe. Europe's military and political power has obviously been reduced in recent years. Yet it would be a mistake to exaggerate her weakness. Europe's inventiveness shows no decline, and the fertility of her artistic imagination is unsurpassed. In the aggregate her economic and military potential is still vast. Her recovery after 1945 is an index to her innate strength. To make this strength count more heavily Western Europe has been taking steps toward economic integration under the prodding of Jean Monnet. (*See Reading No. 32.*) The imaginative Paul-Henri Spaak, Belgian statesman, Chancellor Konrad Adenauer, and others of their broad vision have been working to the same end, with America's blessing. America's example of federalism and Russia's threat of totalitarianism are speeding the day of western Europe's integration.

— 10 —

CONCLUSION

The history of Europe and the rest of the world was radically altered in its course after the age of Columbus and Magellan. Lands hitherto unknown to Europeans came under their influence or direct control. The institutions and technology of Europe were transplanted intact or adapted to new overseas environments. Europe received as well as gave. From Asia she received artistic, literary, and philosophic inspiration as well as silks and spices. Europe's commerce expanded and the revenues of her rulers greatly increased.

European contacts with Asia, however, did not touch deeply the masses of people in either continent. The upper classes and intellectuals of Europe delighted in Chinese philosophy or decorated their homes with furniture and wallpaper designed after Oriental models. The masses of Europe felt the Asian impact only indirectly or not at all. Relatively few Europeans emigrated permanently to Asia.

Overseas expansion entered the consciousness of Europeans when it involved the New World of America. They were more interested in America because their hopes rode with fellow countrymen outward bound. The European whose wish to migrate was defeated lived in two worlds—the Old to which his feet were fixed, the New which housed his dreams. The European whose wish to migrate succeeded also lived for long in two worlds—the Old which housed his past, the New which held his future.

The attachment between western Europe and North America became, in time, very close, closer than that of any other overseas region with the Old World. Europe sent people, capital, and manufactured goods to the New World. The ideas of her artists, educators, scientists, and philosophers fertilized the imaginative life of America.

Migrant Europeans generally chose America above other areas when planning new homes. In these new homes much of the flavor of the Old World was preserved—in language, religion, and cuisine. But the pressures of the new environment effected changes among the immigrants. They learned to talk "American," they were more ready to question political and ecclesiastical authority. Europe's class structure they scorned, and in their pride they pitied all people governed differently from themselves.

Americans felt certain that they were greatly superior to Europeans in handling problems of human relationships. Their readiness to experiment in politics, in penology, in education, drew approving comments from European visitors. American leadership in granting to women rights formerly reserved to men inspired one of the great bloodless revolutions in history. American kindliness and hospitality have been enduring characteristics. America was, in the eyes of close observers, a vast social laboratory in which Old World institutions were tested and preserved, discarded, or transformed.

While Europe watched fascinated, occasionally repelled, it was itself transformed. The democratization of

America from the days of its Revolution influenced the democratization of Europe. This was true not only of Old World politics but also of its class structure, education, and economic well-being. The eventual growth of communications—the inexpensive press, radio, television, magazines, movies—hurried the creation of a transatlantic common culture.

America's moral power continued to maintain its influence over the minds of many, but in time, its economic strength and military potential came to exercise a seemingly greater sway in the calculations of people scattered over the world. A shift in the view of America gradually took place. In earlier years criticism of her came from the right, but in the late nineteenth and twentieth centuries she was dissected by a disillusioned left. Even friendly observers have stressed the dilemma created by the gap between practice and principle in American democracy.

Despite the flaws that members of the Atlantic community have perceived in each other's ways of life, they have come to recognize the basic beliefs that unite them. Chief of these beliefs is faith in democracy and representative institutions that really represent. Hostility to autocracy and to all forms of totalitarianism is the common inheritance of the North Atlantic Civilization.

The free society of the North Atlantic community has twice been preserved in the past forty years by the joint efforts of its members. To maintain it will require further advances toward unity of a Western Europe leagued with North America. The safekeeping of freedom in the modern world lies in the hands of people in the North Atlantic community. They have been the creators of one of the great civilizations in history. They built it with wondrous imagination and by courage and hard work. More such courage and labor, plus hard thinking, will be needed to preserve it.

Part Two

READINGS

— Reading No. 1 —

THE MEANING OF EUROPEAN EXPANSION*

The Atlantic civilization, which is largely the creation of the expansion of Europe, is one of the consequences of the age of discovery and exploration. One of the earliest to appreciate the significance of European expansion and the impact of exotic regions on the Old World was Professor William R. Shepherd of Columbia University

✓   ✓   ✓

The history of the expansion of Europe . . . includes colonization and vastly more. It may be regarded, in fact, as the record of the interpenetration of Europeans and non-Europeans the world over in all departments of human activity. Two fundamental concepts are inherent in its interpretation. Of these the first is that dependencies, other than mere seaports and their restricted hinterland, are the germs of new societies and possibly of new nations. Their inhabitants are communities drawn in greater or less degree from European race stocks, or else composed largely of non-Europeans. In either case they are adapting themselves to a new environment. So far as the Europeans are concerned, the environment is the natural one of the locality into which they have transplanted themselves; whereas the environment for the native peoples is that artificially established for them by the Europeans. This mutuality of environmental operation, European and non-European, works in two ways. It involves an application to native lands and peoples of ideas, institutions, usages and commodities derived from Europe, and determines the extent to which the native type of civilization or bar-

* W. R. Shepherd, "The Expansion of Europe," *Political Science Quarterly*, Vol. XXXIV, pp. 50-51, 211, 406, 408-409. Reprinted by permission of the *Political Science Quarterly*.

barism may be affected. Similarly, in a reverse sense, it connotes the adoption or adaptation by the Europeans of elements drawn from native conditions, both of country and of people, which modify what they have brought from home. Just as the Europeans influence the natives and their surroundings, so in some degree are they themselves influenced.

The second fundamental concept of the expansion of Europe is that whatever Europeans have done oversea and overland beyond their frontiers forms an essential part of the history of their particular nations and of the continent as a whole. The concept is divisible into two phases, of which one may be called the "outward" and the other the "homeward" movement. The former concerns the transmission of European ideas and institutions and the modifications they undergo in contact with their new environment. The latter betokens the results that follow for Europe itself—the influence of such activities upon European civilization proper, and in particular upon the local life and thought of the nations more directly engaged in the work of expansion. Here again a process of interaction is observable. It reveals both the impress made on the civilization of Europe by what the Europeans carry back from their distant ventures, and the manner in which these exotic contributions to European life and thought undergo a change amid new conditions of existence. . . .

Out of the New Worlds in the West and East the achievements of the European have brought forth a New Europe that has continued to speak the languages and cherish the traditions and customs of the former home, that has sought to be freer, richer, more tolerant, less tied to ancient prejudices, more open to progress, and that has served accordingly to influence Old Europe in every phase of its existence. New things have been found, new forms of society created, new kinds of industry devised, new fields of commerce opened up, new opportunities for financial operations discovered, new ideas and new departments of knowledge made manifest and new concepts of national and international welfare evolved, all of which could not fail profoundly to affect Europe itself. Ancient civilizations aroused and energized, primitive beliefs and practices cast into modern molds by the impact of the European, have yielded to him in return many a treasure, material and mental, by which his life and thought have become vastly enriched and diversified. From all that expansion has evoked in spirit and attainment—the zest of enterprise, eagerness for adventure, fame, wealth, new scenes and new homes, new places on the earth where a greater comfort and happiness might be assured, the introduction of the unknown and an increased use of the known—from its contact, in a word, with new lands and new peoples in America, Asia, Africa, and the isles of the sea, Europe has derived new impulses and new developments. . . .

It is the nations fronting on the Atlantic or its immediate backwaters which have profited primarily from the transit overseas of European ideas and institutions. This has meant a tremendous shift in the political balance from central to western Europe. . . .

On internal affairs of a political character in one European country or another oversea interests have frequently exercised a large amount of influence. By them in some degree the modern national states of Europe have been molded out of the feudal monarchies of medieval times. They have served accordingly to furnish the means by which governments could employ salaried officials drawn from the commercial and professional classes, instead of having to depend on feudal agents or functionaries who held their position by right of birth. This circumstance . . . helped to quell the turbulence of clergy and nobility.

— Reading No. 2 —

AMERICAN TREASURE AND THE EUROPEAN ECONOMY*

America's precious metals played an enormously influential role in the life of the Atlantic civilization—in its

* E. J. Hamilton, *American Treasure and the Price Revolution in Spain, 1501-1650* (*Harvard Economic Studies,* Vol. XLIII, Cambridge, Mass., 1934), pp. 33, 34-35, 44-45, 70, 72, 207, 208, 210, 280. Reprinted by permission of the Harvard University Press.

politics, in its literature, in its economy. The ablest student of their impact on Europe's economy is Professor Earl J. Hamilton. From his chief work on this theme a series of selections have been extracted to convey something of the meaning of American wealth for the Old World.

✓   ✓   ✓

The treasure fleets sailed from Spain laden with provisions, wares, and all sorts of merchandise. The return cargo comprised small quantities of colonial produce—such as hides, copper, tobacco, sugar, indigo, and cochineal—and vast sums of silver.

How important this treasure was, how large it loomed in the lives of the Spanish people, can perhaps best be shown by stating that, at the rate prevailing for unskilled labor in Andalusia, the average annual receipts for 1591-1595 would have paid for about twenty-one days' work of all the persons in the country employed for salaries and wages.

For a season industry seems to have responded to the rise in prices precipitated by the influx of treasure. The resultant material prosperity, together with the effect of the specie on national psychology, played a part in the passage of Spain through her golden age of literature and art. . . . Historians have generally agreed that American gold and silver fanned the flames of Hapsburg imperialism, added to the zeal with which Spanish rulers defended the Catholic faith against Protestant and Mohammedan, furnished sinews of war, and, in short, constituted an important factor in Spain's aggressive foreign policy. Furthermore, private treasure, through sequestration upon arrival, contributed very largely to public revenue. And it should be remembered that, because of the relatively undeveloped state of international finance, specie was then highly prized as a means of supporting military operations in distant countries. So gold and silver from the Indies were a factor in the shedding of the blood of Spain—sacrificed on altars of imperialism and religious fanaticism—on distant European battlefields. . . .

One of the most important consequences of the enormous output of the precious metals in the Hispanic colonies of the New World was the complete upsetting of the fairly stable bimetallic ratio which had obtained in the Occident for several centuries.

The imports of American gold and silver into Europe during the sixteenth and the early part of the seventeenth century not only raised prices to approximately the level at which they stood during most of the eighteenth and nineteenth centuries, but raised the mint ratio of gold to silver from approximately 10.00 to 1 . . . to the neighborhood of 15.50 to 1, the approximate center for the oscillations of the next two centuries.

The upheaval of general prices in Spain was incomparably greater than in England. . . . At the zenith, in 1601-1610, Spanish prices were 3.46 times as high as in 1501-1510, while the peak of English prices, in 1643-1652, exceeded the level of 1501-1510 in the ratio of only 2.94 to 1.

Nineteenth- and twentieth-century annals of the leading countries of the Western World afford no example of a hundred-year price upheaval . . . comparable to that which occurred in Spain during the first century of the Price Revolution. If we examine the period 1820-1920, for example, in order to include the peak of the Great War prices, we find that commodity index numbers in the United States rose considerably less than 100 percent, or not half as much proportionately as did those of Spain in the sixteenth century.

From the high-water mark in 1511-1515 to the low-water mark in 1596-1600 the purchasing power of labor time [in Spain] declined almost 30 percent.

BRADFORD AND HIS FELLOW PILGRIMS DECIDE TO GO TO AMERICA*

When William Bradford and his fellow Pilgrims were wrestling with the problem of emigration from Holland, their arguments and objectives were of the type that millions of later emigrants discussed. In Bradford's mind, as in the minds of later migrants, the thought of a happier future for the children is uppermost.

↗   ↗   ↗

As necessitie was a taskmaster over them, so they were forced to be such, not only to their servants, but in a sorte, to their dearest children; the which as it did not a little wound ye tender harts of many a loving father & mother, so it produced likwise sundrie sad & sorowful effects. For many of their children, that were of best dispositions and gracious inclinations, haveing lernde to bear ye yoake in their youth, and willing to bear parte of their parents burden, were, often times, so oppressed with their hevie labours, that though their minds were free and willing, yet their bodies bowed under ye weight of ye same, and became decreped in their early youth; the vigor of nature being consumed in ye very budd as it were. But that which was more lamentable, and of all sorowes most heavie to be borne, was that many of their children, by these occasions, and ye great licentiousnes of youth in yt country, . . . were drawne away by evill examples into extravagante & dangerous courses, getting ye raines off their neks, & departing from their parents. These, & some other like reasons, moved them to undertake this resolution of their removall; the which they afterward prosecuted with so great difficulties. . . .

* William Bradford, *Bradford's History of Plimoth Plantation* (Boston, 1899), pp. 31-35.

The place they had thoughts on was some of those vast & unpeopled countries of America, which are frutfull & fitt for habitation, being devoyd of all civill inhabitants, wher ther are only salvage & brutish men, which range up and downe, litle otherwise then ye wild beasts of the same. This proposition being made publike and coming to ye scaning of all, it raised many variable opinions amongst men, and caused many fears & doubts amongst them selves. Some, from their reasons & hops conceived, laboured to stirr up & incourage the rest to undertake & prosecute ye same; others, againe, out of their fears, objected against it, & sought to diverte from it, aledging many things, and those neither unreasonable nor unprobable; as that it was a great designe, and subjecte to many unconceivable perills & dangers; as, besids the casulties of ye seas . . . the length of ye vioage was such, as ye weake bodys of women and other persons worne out with age & travile . . . could never be able to endure. And yet if they should, the miseries of ye land which they should be exposed unto, would be to hard to be borne; and lickly, some or all of them togeither, to consume & utterly to ruinate them. For ther they should be liable to famine, and nakednes, & ye wante, in a maner, of all things. The chang of aire, diate, & drinking of water, would infecte their bodies with sore sickness, and greevous diseases. And also those which should escape or overcome these difficulties, should yett be in continuall danger of ye salvage people who are cruell, barbarous, & most trecherous, being most furious in their rage, and merciles wher they overcome. . . . And surely it could not be thought but ye very hearing of these things could not but move ye very bowels of men to grate within them, and make ye weake to quake & tremble. It was furder objected, that it would require greater sumes of maney to furnish such a voiage, and to fitt them with necessaries, than their consumed estats would amounte too. . . .

It was answered, that all great & honourable actions are accompanied with great difficulties, and must be both enterprised and overcome with answerable courages. It was granted ye dangers were great, but not desperate; the difficulties were many, but not invincible. . . . True it was, that such atempts were not to be made and undertaken without good ground & reason; not rashly or lightly

as many have done for curiositie or hope of gaine, &c.
But their conditon was not urdinarie; their ends were
good & honourable; their calling lawfull, & urgente; and
therfore they might expecte ye blessing of God in their
proceding. Yea, though they should loose their lives in
this action, yet might they have comforte in the same, and
their endeavors would be honourable. They lived hear
in Holland but as men in exile, & in a poore condition; . . . .

— Reading No. 4 —

FRANKLIN ON AMERICA'S INCREASING NUMBERS AND THEIR VALUE FOR BRITAIN'S ECONOMY*

*Franklin was one of the first to draw attention to
the fact that population growth in America was outsrip-
ping that of Europe. His observations became well known
to Europeans, including Malthus, who made use of them
in their own studies. Franklin's intention was to point out
that the strength of the whole British Empire would be
enhanced by America's growth, but implicit in his remarks is the thought that eventually the greater weight
within the Empire would be wielded by America.*

✓   ✓   ✓

Land being thus plenty in *America,* and so cheap as
that a labouring man, that understands Husbandry, can

* Benjamin Franklin, "Observations concerning the increase
of Mankind, Peopling of Countries, etc.," 1751, in *The
Writings of Benjamin Franklin,* edited by A. H. Smyth
(New York, 1905), Vol. III, pp. 65, 71-72. Reprinted by
permission.

in a short Time save Money enough to purchase a Piece of new Land sufficient for a Plantation, whereon he may subsist a Family, such are not afraid to marry; for, if they even look far enough forward to consider how their Children, when grown up, are to be provided for, they see that more Land is to be had at rates equally easy, all Circumstances considered.

Hence Marriages in *America* are more general, and more generally early, than in *Europe*. And if it is reckoned there, that there is but one Marriage per Annum among 100 persons, perhaps we may here reckon two; and if in Europe they have but 4 Births to a Marriage (many of their Marriages being late), we may here reckon 8, of which if one half grow up, and our Marriages are made, reckoning one with another at 20 Years of Age, our People must at least be doubled every 20 Years.

But notwithstanding this Increase, so vast is the Territory of *North America,* that it will require many Ages to settle it fully; and, till it is fully settled, Labour will never be cheap here, where no Man continues long a Labourer for others, but gets a Plantation of his own, no Man continues long a Journeyman to a Trade, but goes among those new Settlers, and sets up for himself, &c. Hence Labour is no cheaper now in *Pennsylvania,* than it was 30 Years ago, tho' so many Thousand labouring People have been imported. . . .

Thus there are suppos'd to be now upwards of One Million *English* Souls in *North-America,* (tho' 'tis thought scarce 80,000 have been brought over Sea,) and yet perhaps there is not one the fewer in *Britain,* but rather many more, on Account of the Employment the Colonies afford to Manufacturers at Home. This Million doubling, suppose but once in 25 Years, will, in another Century, be more than the People of *England,* and the greatest Number of *Englishmen* will be on this Side the Water. What an Accession of Power to the *British* Empire by Sea as well as Land! What Increase of Trade and Navigation! What Numbers of Ships and Seamen! We have been here but little more than 100 years, and yet the Force of our Privateers in the late War, united, was greater, both in Men and Guns, than that of the whole *British* Navy in Queen *Elizabeth's* Time. How important an Affair then to *Britain* is the present Treaty for settling the Bounds between her Colonies and the *French,* and how careful should she be to secure Room enough, since on the Room depends so much the Increase of her People. . . . If you have Room and Subsistence enough . . . you may of one make ten Nations, equally populous and powerful; or rather increase a Nation ten fold in Numbers and Strength.

— Reading No. 5 —

THE RELIGIOUS REVIVAL IN THE 18TH CENTURY*

The Rev. George Whitefield was a leading figure on both sides of the Atlantic in the religious revival of the 1730's and the years thereafter. His fame in England brought him invitations to America where his influence was immense. This report of his activities, by the Rev. Thomas Prince of Boston is relatively restrained, neither hostile nor overenthusiastic. Others were more partisan.

From the year 1738, we had received accounts of the rev. Mr. Whitefield, as a very pious young minister of the church of England, rising up in the spirit of the reformers, and preaching their doctrines first in England, and then in America, with surprising power and success; which raised desires in great numbers among us to see and hear him. And having received invitations to come hither, he from Georgia and South-Carolina arrived at Rhode-Island on the Lord's-day, September 14, 1740, and the Thursday evening after came to Boston. Next day Dr. Sewall and I

* John Gillies, *Historical Collections relating to remarkable periods of The Success of The Gospel* (Glasgow, 1754, 2 vols.), II, pp. 163-165.

made him a visit, found several ministers and other gentlemen of the town with him, and that Dr. Colman and Mr. Cooper had engaged him to preach this afternoon in their house of public worship; and in about an hour we went to the place, which quickly crowded with two or three thousand people. . . . He spake as became the oracles of God in demonstration of the Spirit and of power; and especially when he came to his application, he addressed himself to the audience in such a tender, earnest, and moving manner, exciting us to come and be acquainted with the dear Redeemer, as melted the assembly into tears.

Next morning, at Dr. Sewall's and my desire, he preached at the South-church to further acceptance. . . . And though now and then he dropped some expressions that were not so accurate and guarded as we should expect from aged and long-studied ministers, yet I had the satisfaction to observe his readiness with great modesty and thankfulness to receive correction as soon as offered. In short, he was a most importunate wooer of souls to come to Christ for the enjoyment of him and all his benefits. He distinctly applied his exhortations to the elderly people, the middle-aged, the young, the Indians, and Negroes; and a most winning way of addressing them. . . .

Multitudes were greatly affected, and many awakened with his lively ministry. Though he preached every day, the houses were exceedingly crowded; but when he preached in the Common, a vaster number attended: and almost every evening the house where he lodged was thronged to hear his prayers and counsels. Upon invitation he also preached in several neighbouring towns, travelled and preached as far as York, above seventy miles north-east of Boston, returned hither . . . next . . . travelled westward to Northampton, thence through Connecticut, New-York, and New-Jersey to Philadelphia, and thence sailed to South-Carolina.

Upon his leaving us, great numbers in this town were so happily concerned about their souls, as we had never seen anything like it before . . . and their desires excited to hear their ministers more than ever; so that our assemblies, both on lectures and Sabbaths, were surprizingly increased, and now the people wanted to hear us oftner . . .

Upon the Rev. Mr. Gilbert Tennent's coming and preaching here, the people appeared to be yet much more awakened about their souls than before . . . his preaching was as searching and rouzing as ever I heard.

— Reading No. 6 —

THOMAS HOLLIS SENDS BOOKS TO AMERICA*

The cultural relations between the Old World and the New were fostered by the dispatch of books from Europe. Individuals and institutions bought many and begged for more, and no one was more generous in response than Thomas Hollis. He was anxious that colonials read with a purpose—the enlargement of civil and religious liberty.

Bountiful as he was to the American Colonies, it was not a partial and exclusive love, or what is called a *predilection,* that influenced his conduct in the choice of his presents. He sent them, not what he thought might be most acceptable to particular persons, but what he judged from their progress in literary or scientific improvement might be most useful to the community. And this he did to other countries, where he understood the cultivation of literature and science was in repute, and was the employment of their seminaries and societies; . . . it is manifest, from the various learning contained in the volumes he sent them, that the enlargement of their notions of civil and religious liberty was not the least part of his design.

Perhaps there never went from his hands, by way of present, the smallest pamphlet, or the minutest article of virtù, without some particular view to the advancement of the reputation and honour of his native country.

* *Memoirs of Thomas Hollis, Esq.* (London, 1780), vi.

LA ROCHEFOUCAULD-LIANCOURT ON AMERICAN PRISONS*

From the end of the eighteenth century until well down into the nineteenth, Europeans were deeply interested in American penology. Americans had studied European reformers, notably John Howard, but they felt they had something to contribute beyond what had been attempted in the Old World. In this humanitarian endeavor, as in others, their inventiveness was commended to Europe by Old World visitors.

✔   ✔   ✔

The gaoler is not here, as is too often the case in Europe, an extortioner, who lays under contribution the weakness, the captivity, and the misery of the confined. No garnish, no purchase of favours, or privileges, no dismission fees disgrace these prisons. In Europe the small salary annexed to many places seem to authorise the holder of them to extend his revenues. And it is certainly very difficult for a superior officer, who knows that the appointments of such persons do not afford them a proper livelihood, not to wink at many of the methods employed, by each one respectively, to procure himself a better subsistence. . . . This species of greedy extortion seems to belong, in a peculiar manner, to the degraded classes of society. It is a kind of vengeance exercised by those who have learnt to be indifferent to the esteem of others, in return for the contempt with which they are treated by the world.

The success of the new system, is on the point, therefore, of being more complete than Howard himself had ventured to contemplate: for he considered the hope, that the labour of prisoners would ever defray the expences of

* From Duke de La Rochefoucauld-Liancourt, *On the Prisons of Philadelphia* (Philadelphia, 1796), pp. 14-15, 31, 33.

their detention as an illusion; And yet, those in the gaol of Philadelphia, on their dismission, besides paying their expences of every kind, take with them an overplus of profit. His opinion was, likewise, that fetters, and whipping, were indispensable in the management of prisoners; and yet, all corporal correction, as well as irons, are forbidden in this gaol. And lastly, the punishment of death, which, according to Howard, the law still to inflict on house-breakers, incendiaries, and murderers in general, is confined here to murders of the first degree.

May the new continent, accustomed to receive from Europe, that illumination, which her youth and inexperience require, serve, in her turn, as a model, to reform the criminal jurisprudence, and establish a new system of imprisonment, in the old world; severe, and terrible, yet humane and just. To America, it must be confessed, we are indebted for the first example. The opinions that gave it birth, are doubtless of European origin. . . . But the attempt at an almost entire abolition of the punishment of death, and the substitution of a system of reason and justice, to that of bonds, ill-treatment, and arbitrary punishment, was never made but in America. The obstacles, to such an attempt, it must be acknowledged, are in Europe, almost unsurmountable. But they were not small even in this country. . . . The prejudices of most men were opposed to the innovation; and, notwithstanding this, the courage and perseverance of a few citizens, terminated in triumph.

— Reading No. 8 —

THE IMPACT OF THE AMERICAN REVOLUTION UPON EUROPE*

Among the notable figures in Europe who measured the significance of the American Revolution for the rest

* Oeuvres Complètes de Condorcet (Brunswick, 1804), Tome XI, pp. 251, 252-253, 255, 260.

of the world was the French philosophe, *Condorcet. He wrote an essay,* On the Influence of the American Revolution upon Europe, *which expressed his hopes that the Old World would be instructed by the New.*

✓   ✓   ✓

The spectacle of a great people among whom the rights of man are respected is useful to all others, in spite of the difference in climate, customs, and constitutions. It is understood that these rights are everywhere the same. . . .

If America had succumbed to the arms of England, despotism would also have forged its chains on the mother country. . . .

Liberty of the press is established in America where it is justly considered that the right to speak and to hear the truth . . . is one of the most sacred rights of mankind. . . .

The spectacle of equality which obtains in the United States, and which assures peace and prosperity, can also be useful to Europe.

— Reading No. 9 —

THOMAS POWNALL ON AMERICAN LIBERTY*

Pownall's service in America acquainted him with the spirit of the people, which he understood perhaps better than any other British official. He and Franklin were friends and collaborated on projects for strengthening the

* Thomas Pownall, *A Memorial Addressed to the Sovereigns of America* (London, 1783), pp. 54, 55, 56, 57, 137-138.

*Empire. He had a keen understanding of the future bene-
fits to the world of Anglo-American cooperation. Like
Franklin, he was truly an Atlantic citizen.*

✓   ✓   ✓

The Liberty of the People of America is not merely
that share of Power, which an Aristocracy permits the
People to amuse themselves with, and which they are
taught to call Liberty. It is not that Domination with which
the People govern in a Democracy, and therefore call
Liberty. It is not that share of Domination which a political Monarch throws into the hands of the People,
in order to ally their power to his Force, by which to
govern the Aristocracy. The genuine Liberty on which
America is founded is totally and intirely a New System
of Things and Men, which treats all as what they actually
are, esteeming nothing the True End and perfect Good
of Policy but that Effect which produces, as equality of
Rights, so equal Liberty, universal Peace, and unob-
structed intercommunion of happiness in Human Society.

Every Inhabitant of America is, *de facto* as well as *de
jure,* equal, in his essential inseparable rights of the individual, to any other Individual; is, in these rights, independent of any power that any other can assume over him,
over his labour or his property: This is a Principle in act
and deed, and not a mere speculative Theorem. He is
his own master both in his reasoning and acting; so far
as respects the individual, he is at perfect liberty to apply his power as he likes, to labour in any line, and to
possess and use his property as his own. His property is
free from any tenure or condition that may clog, obstruct,
or divert the fruits of that labour which he hath mixt
with it.

There are not in this Land of Liberty any Feudal, any
Personal services, which may be claimed by a Landlord
from the Landholder, . . . neither as a Labourer, nor
as a Landworker, does the American ever find himself
crossed upon by any of those self-obstructive Policies,
which have been the bane to Industry, and blasted the
fruits of labour in Europe.

In America, Love and Liberty go hand in hand; and
each individual forms those connections which nature and

the heart point out. Marriage there is a Civil Contract, which is contracted, remains obligatory, or is dissoluble, just as any other Civil Contract is.

Let them [Americans] remember . . . that by a free commerce they diffuse to the World at large the surplus portion of these good things which they must be continually creating in their own World; that they consider themselves as the means in the hands of Providence, of extending the Civilization of human Society; and the Teachers, by their example, of those Political Truths, which are meant, not to enslave, but to render men more free and happy under Government. If they take up this Character within themselves, and hold out its operations and effect to the Old World, they will become a Nation *to whom all Nations will come;* a Power whom all the Powers of Europe will court to Civil and Commercial Alliances; a People to whom the Remnants of all ruined People will fly, whom all the oppressed and injured of every nation will seek to for refuge. *The riches of the Sea will pour in upon them; the wealth of Nations must flow in upon them;* and they must be a populous and Rich People.

— Reading No. 10 —

WHAT IS AN AMERICAN?*

European visitors to America and natives of the colonies themselves were conscious of the growing differences in living, on both sides of the Atlantic. No one better expressed that difference than Crèvecoeur, the trans-

* J. Hector St. John Crèvecoeur, *Letters from an American Farmer* (London, 1782; reprinted New York, 1925), pp. 49, 50, 51, 52-53, 54-56. Reprinted by permission of Albert and Charles Bowi, Inc.

planted Frenchman who became famous as the author of Letters from an American Farmer.

⁋   ⁋   ⁋

What a train of pleasing ideas this fair spectacle must suggest; it is a prospect which must inspire a good citizen with the most heartfelt pleasure. The difficulty consists in the manner of viewing so extensive a scene. He is arrived on a new continent; a modern society offers itself to his contemplation, different from what he had hitherto seen. It is not composed, as in Europe, of great lords who possess every thing, and of a herd of people who have nothing. Here are no aristocratical families, no courts, no kings, no bishops, no ecclesiastical dominion, no invisible power giving to a few a very visible one; no great manufacturers employing thousands, no great refinements of luxury. The rich and the poor are not so far removed from each other as they are in Europe. Some few towns excepted, we are all tillers of the earth, from Nova Scotia to West Florida. We are a people of cultivators, scattered over an immense territory, communicating with each other by means of good roads and navigable rivers, united by the silken bands of mild government, all respecting the laws, without dreading their power, because they are equitable. . . .

If [one] travels through our rural districts he views not the hostile castle, and the haughty mansion, contrasted with the clay-built hut and miserable cabbin, where cattle and men help to keep each other warm, and dwell in meanness, smoke, and indigence. A pleasing uniformity of decent competence appears throughout our habitations. The meanest of our log-houses is a dry and comfortable habitation. Lawyer or merchant are the fairest titles our towns afford; that of a farmer is the only appellation of the rural inhabitants of our country. . . . We have no princes, for whom we toil, starve, and bleed: we are the most perfect society now existing in the world. Here man is free as he ought to be; nor is this pleasing equality so transitory as many others are. . . .

The next wish of this traveller will be to know whence came all these people? they are a mixture of English, Scotch, Irish, French, Dutch, Germans, and Swedes. From this promiscuous breed, that race now called Americans have arisen. . . .

In this great American asylum, the poor of Europe have by some means met together, and in consequence of various causes; to what purpose should they ask one another what countrymen they are? Alas, two thirds of them had no country. Can a wretch who wanders about, who works and starves, whose life is a continual scene of sore affliction or pinching penury; can that man call England or any other kingdom his country? A country that had no bread for him, whose fields procured him no harvest, who met with nothing but the frowns of the rich, the severity of the laws, with jails and punishments; who owned not a single foot of the extensive surface of this planet? No! urged by a variety of motives, here they came. Every thing has tended to regenerate them; new laws, a new mode of living, a new social system; here they are become men: in Europe they were as so many useless plants, wanting vegetative mould, and refreshing showers; they withered, and were mowed down by want, hunger, and war; but now by the power of transplantation, like all other plants they have taken root and flourished! Formerly they were not numbered in any civil lists of their country, except in those of the poor; here they rank as citizens. By what invisible power has this surprising metamorphosis been performed? By that of the laws and that of their industry. The laws, the indulgent laws, protect them as they arrive, stamping on them the symbol of adoption; they receive ample rewards for their labours; these accumulated rewards procure them lands; those lands confer on them the title of freemen, and to that title every benefit is affixed which men can possible require. This is the great operation daily performed by our laws. From whence proceed these laws? From our government. Whence the government? It is derived from the original genius and strong desire of the people ratified and confirmed by the crown. This is the great chain which links us all, this is the picture which every province exhibits. . . .

What then is the American, this new man? He is either an European, or the descendant of an European, hence that strange mixture of blood, which you will find in no other country. I could point out to you a family whose grandfather was an Englishman, whose wife was Dutch, whose son married a French woman, and whose present four sons have now four wives of different nations. *He* is an American, who leaving behind him all his ancient prejudices and manners, receives new ones from the new mode of life he has embraced, the new government he obeys, and the new rank he holds. He becomes an American by being received in the broad lap of our great *Alma Mater*. Here individuals of all nations are melted into a new race of men, whose labours and posterity will one day cause great changes in the world. Americans are the western pilgrims, who are carrying along with them that great mass of arts, sciences, vigour, and industry which began long since in the east; they will finish the great circle. The Americans were once scattered all over Europe; here they are incorporated into one of the finest systems of population which has ever appeared, and which will hereafter become distinct by the power of the different climates they inhabit. The American ought therefore to love this country much better than that wherein either he or his forefathers were born. Here the rewards of his industry follow with equal steps the progress of his labour; his labour is founded on the basis of nature, *self-interest;* can it want a stronger allurement? Wives and children, who before in vain demanded of him a morsel of bread, now, fat and frolicsome, gladly help their father to clear those fields whence exuberant crops are to arise to feed and to clothe them all; without any part being claimed, either by a despotic prince, a rich abbot, or a mighty lord. Here religion demands but little of him; a small voluntary salary to the minister, and gratitude to God; can he refuse these? The American is a new man, who acts upon new principles; he must therefore entertain new ideas, and form new opinions. From involuntary idleness, servile dependence, penury, and useless labour, he has passed to toils of a very different nature, rewarded by ample subsistence.—This is an American.

— Reading No. 11 —

RICHARD PRICE ON THE IMPORTANCE OF THE AMERICAN REVOLUTION*

Richard Price, a well-known Dissenting clergyman of liberal views, was a close friend of Franklin and of the American cause. He had many correspondents among leading Americans, whose views he communicated to the English public. His ardent support of the American Revolution led him to write a short work on the meaning of that great event for the world.

✓   ✓   ✓

The late war, in its *commencement* and *progress,* did great good by disseminating just sentiments of the rights of mankind, and the nature of legitimate government; by exciting a resistance to tyranny, which has emancipated one *European* country, and is likely to emancipate others; and by occasioning the establishment in *America* of forms of government more equitable and more liberal than any that the world has yet known. But, in its *termination,* the war has done still greater good by preserving the new governments from that destruction in which they must have been involved, had Britain conquered; by providing, in a sequestered continent possessed of many singular advantages, a place of refuge for opprest men in every region of the world; and by laying the foundation there of an empire which may be the seat of liberty, science and virtue, and from whence there is reason to hope these sacred blessings will spread, till they become universal and the time arrives when kings and priests shall have no more power to op-

* Richard Price, *On the Importance of the American Revolution and the Means of Making It a Benefit to Mankind* (London, 1784; reprinted in Boston, 1784), pp 4, 7, 84.

press, and that ignominious slavery which has hitherto debased the world is exterminated.

Perhaps, I do not go too far when I say that, next to the introduction of Christianity among mankind, the American revolution may prove to be the most important step in the progressive course of human improvement. It is an event which may produce a general diffusion of the principles of humanity, and become the means of setting free mankind from the shackles of superstition and tyranny, by leading them to see and know. . . . "That the members of a civil community are *confederates,* not *subjects;* and their rulers, *servants,* not *masters."*

[*At the end of Price's pamphlet is a letter to him from Turgot, a very influential figure in French politics in the era of the American Revolution. Turgot, like Price, was a strong admirer of America, and hoped she would avoid the faults of the Old World. The letter was dated Paris, March 22, 1778.*]

It [America] is the hope of the human race. It may become their model. It should prove to the world in fact that men may be free and tranquil, and may rid themselves from the many shackles which tyrants and impostures of every garb have endeavoured to impose on them, under a pretext of the public good. It should give an example of political freedom, of religious freedom, of the freedom of commerce and of industry. The asylum which it opens to all the oppressed of all nations, ought to console the whole earth. The facility of taking advantage of this to get free from the effects of bad governments will oblige such governments to grow just and enlightened; and the rest of the world will by degrees open their eyes upon that bubble of illusions wherein politicians have lulled themselves.

— Reading No. 12 —

JEFFERSON ON EUROPEAN VS. AMERICAN EDUCATION*

Jefferson may be pictured as a strong nationalist, the usual characterization, or as one who was anxious that Americans share in the best that Europe had to offer without losing any of their own distinctiveness. On the subject of education, especially, he was careful to emphasize the virtues of the Old World and the New, desiring always that young people should have the best of both worlds. Jefferson was answering a query as to the best seminary for youth in Europe.

The result of these [inquiries] has been to consider the competition as resting between Geneva and Rome. . . . The advantage of Geneva is, that students acquire there the habit of speaking French. The advantages of Rome are the acquiring a local knowledge of a spot so classical and so celebrated; the acquiring the true pronuntiation of the Latin language; the acquiring a just taste in the fine arts, more particularly those of painting, sculpture, Architecture, and Music; a familiarity with those objects and processes of agriculture which experience has shewn best adapted to a climate like ours; and lastly, the advantage of a fine climate for health. . . . I think the balance in favor of Rome. . . . But why send an American youth to Europe for education? What are the objects of an useful American education? Classical knowledge, modern languages. . . . Mathematics, Natural philosophy, Natural history, Civil History; Ethics. In Natural philosophy,

* *The Papers of Thomas Jefferson,* Julian P. Boyd, editor (Princeton 1950-   ), Vol. 8, pp. 568-569, 635-638: Jefferson to Charles Bellini, Sept. 30, 1785; Jefferson to John Banister, Jr., Oct. 15, 1785. Reprinted by permission of Princeton University Press.

I mean to include Chemistry and Agriculture, and in Natural history, to include Botany, as well as the other branches of those departments. It is true that the habit of speaking the modern languages cannot be so well acquired in America; but every other article can be as well acquired at William and Mary College, as at any place in Europe. When College education is done with, and a young man is to prepare himself for public life, he must cast his eyes (for America) either on Law or Physic [medicine]. For the former, where can he apply so advantageously as to Mr. Wythe? [*Wythe was Jefferson's teacher at William and Mary*] For the latter [medicine] he must come to Europe; the medical class of students, therefore, is the only one which need come to Europe. Let us view the disadvantages of sending a youth to Europe. To enumerate them all, would require a volume. I will select a few. If he goes to England, he learns drinking, horse racing, and boxing. . . . The following circumstances are common to education in that and the other countries of Europe. He acquires a fondness for European luxury and dissipation and a contempt for the simplicity of his own country; he is fascinated with the privileges of the European aristocrats, and sees with abhorrence the lovely equality which the poor enjoy with the rich in his own country; . . . he forms foreign friendships which will never be useful to him, and loses the seasons of life for forming in his own country those friendships which of all others are the most faithful and permanent; he is led, by the strongest of all the human passions, into . . . intrigue . . . [with] whores; . . . he retains, thro' life a fond recollection and a hankering after those places, which were the scenes of his first pleasures and of his first connections; he returns to his own country, a foreigner, unacquainted with the practices of domestic economy, necessary to preserve him from ruin. . . . It appears to me then that an American coming to Europe for education loses in his knowledge, in his morals, in his health, in his habits, and in his happiness. I had entertained only doubts on this head before I came to Europe: what I see and hear since I came here proves more than I had even suspected. Cast your eye over America: who are the men of most learning, of most eloquence, most beloved by their country and most trusted and promoted by them? They are those who have been educated among them, and whose manners, morals, and habits, are perfectly homogeneous with those of the country.

[*To Mr. Bellini.*] Behold me at length on the vaunted scene of Europe! It is not necessary for your information, that I should enter into details concerning it. But you are, perhaps, curious to know how this new scene has struck a savage of the mountains of America. Not advantageously, I assure you. I find the general fate of humanity here most deplorable. The truth of Voltaire's observation, offers itself perpetually, that every man here must be either the hammer or the anvil. It is a true picture of that country to which they say we shall pass hereafter, and where we are to see god and his angels in splendor, and crowds of the damned trampled under their feet. While the great mass of the people are thus suffering under physical and moral oppression, I have endeavored to examine more nearly the condition of the great, to appreciate the true value of the circumstances in their situation which dazzle the bulk of spectators, and especially to compare it with that degree of happiness which is enjoyed in America by every class of people. . . .

In science, the mass of the people is two centuries behind ours; their literati, half a dozen years before us. Books, really good, acquire just reputation in that time, and so become known to us and communicate to us all their advances in knowledge. . . . With respect to what are termed polite manners, . . . I would wish [my] countrymen to adopt just so much of European politeness as to be ready [to] make all those little sacrifices of self which really render European manners amiable, and relieve society from the disagreeable scenes to which rudeness often exposes it. . . . In the pleasures of the table they are far before us, because with good taste they unite temperance. They do not terminate the most sociable meals by transforming themselves into brutes. I have never yet seen a man drunk in France, even among the lowest of the people. Were I to proceed to tell you how much I enjoy their architecture, sculpture, painting, music, I should want words. It is in these arts they shine. The last of them, particularly, is an enjoiment, the deprivation of which with us, cannot be calculated. I am almost ready to say, it is the only thing which from my heart I envy them, and which in spight of all the authority of the decalogue, I do covet. But I am running on in an estimate of things infinitely better known to you than to me, and which will only serve to convince you, that I have brought with me all the prejudices of country, habit and age. . . .

— Reading No. 13 —

PROPHECIES OF AMERICA'S GREATNESS*

Many Europeans foretold the eventual rise of America to greatness. These prophecies were connected with a familiar tradition that spoke of declining civilizations in the East and rising societies in the West. The fact of America's vigor and her geographic location, west of Europe, confirmed many in their belief in the destiny of the New World. Bishop Berkeley's "Verses on the Prospect of Planting Arts and Learning in America" (1726) were among the first, and most famous, lines on this theme. In the Revolutionary era such prophecies increased greatly.

✓   ✓   ✓

Westward the course of empire takes its way;
   The first four acts already past,
A fifth shall close the drama with the day;
   Time's noblest offspring is the last.

An idea, strange as it is visionary, has entered into the minds of the generality of mankind, that empire is travelling westward; and every one is looking forward with eager and impatient expectation to that destined

* Charles Sumner, *Prophetic Voices Concerning America* (Boston, 1874), pp. 24, 26, 42, 43, 45, 106, 142, 143.

moment when America is to give the law to the rest of the world. [A. Burnaby, *Travels through the Middle Settlements of North America, in 1759 and 1760.*]

⸲ [*Turgot to Josiah Tucker, the English economist, 1770.*] As a citizen of the world, I see with joy the approach of an event which, more than all the books of philosophers, will dissipate the phantom of commercial jealousy. I mean the separation of your colonies from the mother country, WHICH WILL BE FOLLOWED SOON BY THAT OF ALL AMERICA FROM EUROPE. It is then that the discovery of this part of the world will become to us truly useful. It is then that it will multiply our enjoyments much more abundantly than when we purchased them with torrents of blood.

[*Turgot, April, 1776.*] The present war will probably end in the absolute independence of the colonies, and that event will certainly be *the epoch of the greatest revolution in the commerce and politics not of England only, but of all Europe. . . .* When the English themselves shall recognize the independence of their colonies, *every mother country will be forced* in like manner to exchange its dominion over its colonies for bonds of friendship and fraternity. . . . When the *total separation of America* shall have healed the European nations of the jealousy of commerce, there will exist among men the great cause of war the less, and it is very difficult not to desire an event which is to accomplish this good for the human race.

[*Turgot to Richard Price, 1778.*] It [America] is the hope of the human race. It can become its model. It must prove to the world . . . that men can be free and tranquil, and can dispense with the chains of all kinds which the tyrants and charlatans of every cloth have pretended to impose under the pretext of public good. It must give the example of political liberty, of religious liberty, of commercial and industrial liberty. The asylum which it opens to the oppressed of all nations must console the earth. The facility it affords for escape from a bad government will force the European governments to be just and enlightened. The rest of the world, little by little, will open their eyes to the nothingness of the illusions in which politicians have nursed them. To this end it is necessary that America should take guaranties, and should not become . . . an image of Europe, *a heap of divided Powers,* disputing about territory or commercial profits, and continually cementing the slavery of people with their own blood.

[*The Abbé Galiani, of Naples, to a correspondent, May, 1776.*] Do you know the reality? *The epoch has come of the total fall of Europe, and of transmigration into America.* All here turns into rottenness,—religions, laws, arts, sciences,—and all hastens to renew itself in America. . . . I have said it, announced it, preached it, for more than twenty years, and I have constantly seen my prophecies come to pass. *Therefore, do not buy your house in the Chausée d'Antin;* [Paris] *you must buy it in Philadelphia.* My trouble is that there are no abbeys in America.

[*Count Aranda to the King of Spain, 1783.*] *This Federal Republic is born a pygmy,* so to speak. It required the support and the forces of two powers as great as Spain and France in order to attain independence. *A day will come when it will be a giant, even a colossus formidable in these countries.* It will then forget the benefits which it has received from the two powers, and will dream of nothing but to organize itself. *Liberty of conscience, the facility for establishing a new population on immense lands, as well as the advantages of the new government, will draw thither agriculturists and artisans from all the nations; for men always run after fortune. . . . And in a few years we shall see with true grief the tyrannical existence of this same colossus of which I speak.*

The first movement of this power, when it has arrived at its aggrandizement, will be to obtain possession of the Floridas, in order to dominate the Gulf of Mexico. After having rendered commerce with New Spain difficult for us, it will aspire to the conquest of this vast empire, which it will not be possible for us to defend against a formidable power established on the same continent, and in its neighborhood. These fears are well founded, Sire; they will be changed into reality in a few years, if, indeed, there are not other disorders in our Americas still more fatal. . . .

Your Majesty must relieve yourself of all your possessions on the continent of the two Americas, *preserving only the islands of Cuba and Porto Rico* in the northern part, and some other convenient one in the southern part, to serve as a seaport or trading-place for Spanish commerce.

— Reading No. 14 —

AMERICA SHIFTS THE CENTER OF GRAVITY IN THE ATLANTIC WORLD*

Pownall was more aware than others of the significance of the United States in altering the relationships of the powers bordering on the Atlantic. His was a remarkable forecast of what came to pass with startling consequences in the twentieth century.

✓ ✓ ✓

North America is become *a new primary planet* in the system of the world, which, whilst it takes its own course in its own orbit, must have effect on the orbit of every other planet and SHIFT the common centre of gravity of the whole system of the European world.

There are at present, in perfect independence, two sovereign states in the Atlantic, who . . . are especially and peculiarly Atlantic; and still more are naturally, if not politically allied, by that intercommunion and union which this Atlantic interest creates between them. Great Britain on the east of that ocean, and the United States on the west, both of the same family and tongue . . . ; both having and enjoying the same principles of freedom, the same form of political constitution, as far as the differing circumstances of each admit. These two are by nature formed to become constituents of a FAMILY COMPACT. . . .

There is nothing which would more strongly cement this alliance between these two Atlantic powers, than their joining . . . [to] emancipate the inhabitants of the Spanish provinces in South America . . . and . . . lay-

* Thomas Pownall, *Memorial Addressed to the Sovereigns of Europe and the Atlantic* (London, 1803), pp. 9, 67-68, 73-74.

ing open the abundantly rich commerce of those regions *to the free intercourse of all the world.* . . . The joint operations of those two Atlantic powers, in actuating this commerce, will create a new Atlantic common interest, by raising into freedom and independence an Atlantic state; and that state must, from its own nature, and from the relations which it holds to these its deliverers and defenders, become an acting party in, and give additional strength to, the GREAT MARINE ATLANTIC ALLIANCE.

— Reading No. 15 —

A PLEA FOR ANGLO-AMERICAN SOLIDARITY, 1854 *

Everyone is familiar with the story of friction between the United States and England in the decades following the Revolution. Yet there is a countertheme which stressed the need for collaboration. The emphasis is on the common heritage of both peoples and their necessity to stand together against absolutism. The date of this selection, it will be noted, is that of the Crimean War.

✓   ✓   ✓

In these times, when the influence of Race is becoming so acknowledged in the world's history . . . there is little probability . . . of any one undervaluing the bond of relationship which links the British nation to their fellow-race of Anglo-Saxons in America. The same in blood, we are the same also in the spirit of our institutions. . . . [Many Britons have recently gone to America, creating new ties, and new inventions are bringing the two people closer together.] New York is as near to us now as . . . Edinburgh [was] to London in the boyhood of our fathers. . . . Were the eventualities of the war to

* *Littel's Living Age* (1854), Vol. XLII, p. 243, from the *Dublin Universal Magazine.*

demand it, a military expedition . . . could cross from the New World to the Old with as little difficulty as our fathers equipped the expedition to Flanders. . . .

There has been arising a peril for Freedom and Civilization, which it may be doubted if anything short of a union of these two Powers will suffice to resist. . . . [Absolutism has been strengthening itself in Europe, except in England.] Day by day the Continent, swayed by its despots, is becoming more alien to us in spirit. [The two free Anglo-Saxon empires must stick together. American sympathy for Russia is a mistake. If America seeks now to benefit from England's temporary crisis, by going along with Russia and expanding her empire at Spain's expense, and ignoring ties of race with England, she may yet meet with a bad fate. America can expand to the Isthmus of Panama peacefully; her imperial role in the New World is taken for granted; England and America together must] stand up for freedom and Anglo-Saxonism throughout the world. [They are not rivals; England's true interests lie to the east; each can render assistance to the other in their respective spheres of interest.] As the present war rolls on, England will find herself wholly severed from her Continental alliances. In such an hour of isolation she will need the support of her colonies, both old and young—and we know that she will have it. And then —and this is the great object of our anxiety—let not our own present policy, or that of the United States be such as to render that future alliance impossible or *too late*.

— Reading No. 16 —

*THE EDINBURGH REVIEW
AND AMERICA* *

The Edinburgh Review *has an unpleasant reputation among Americans for its supposed hostility to the young*

* *The Edinburgh Review* (1820), Vol. XXXIII, pp. 397-414.

Republic. But it was not always critical, and in the following selection it made a special effort to emphasize its friendliness to America. It raised the question, what should be the attitude of England and America toward each other?

✓   ✓   ✓

As to the mother country . . . without claiming for her any romantic tenderness or generosity . . . we think we may say, that she oppressed and domineered over them [colonies] much less than any other modern nation has done over such settlements—that she allowed them for the most part, liberal charters and constitutions . . . although she did manifest . . . a disposition to encroach on their privileges, their rights were, on the whole, very tolerably respected—so that they grew up to a state of prosperity, and a familiarity with freedom . . . which was not only without parallel in any similar establishments, but probably could not have been attained had they been earlier left to their own guidance and protection. This is all that we ask for England, on a review of her colonial policy, and her conduct before the war; and this, we think, no candid and well-informed person can reasonably refuse her. . . .

It is a fact which can require no proof, even in America, that there is a party in this country not friendly to political liberty, and decidedly hostile to all extension of popular rights. . . . Now, it is quite true that *this Party* dislikes America, and is apt enough to decry and insult her. Its adherents never have forgiven the success of her war of independence . . . her supposed rivalry in trade—and above all, the happiness and tranquility which she enjoys under a republican form of government. Such a spectacle of democratical prosperity is unspeakably mortifying to their high monarchical principles, and is easily imagined to be dangerous to their security . . . the splendid and steady success of the freest and most popular form of government that ever was established in the world, must have struck the most lively alarm into the hearts of all those who were anxious to have it believed that the People could never interfere in politics but to their ruin. . . . [But the people of England are glad of opportunity to throw the example of New World into the faces of reactionaries in the Old. Ties between people on both sides of Atlantic rest on ideological grounds as well as on trade. A great contest impends in the Old World.]

In Germany, Spain, France, Italy, the principle of Reform and Liberty are visibly arraying themselves for a final struggle with the principles of Established Abuse,—Legitimacy, of Tyranny. . . . [Much will depend on the part that is taken by America.] Her great and growing wealth and population—her universal commercial relations—her own impregnable security—and her remoteness from the scene of dissension—must give her prodigious power and influence in such a crisis, either as a mediator or umpire, or . . . as an auxiliary and ally. [America might stand aloof because of anger against England because of the actions of a few calumnious individuals. But their common inheritance of freedom should put them on the same side in this fight.] Had England not been free, the worst despotism in Europe must have been far worse than it is, at this moment. [But English strength is not great enough.] It is in aid of this decaying, perhaps expiring influence—it is as an associate or successor in the noble [effort] . . . of patronizing and protecting general liberty, that we call upon America to throw from her the memory of all petty differences . . . and to unite herself cordially with the liberal and enlightened part of the English nation; . . . their disunion will give dreadful advantages to the enemies of all improvement and reform. The *example* of America has already done much for that cause; and the very existence of such a country, under such a government, is a tower of strength, and a standard of encouragement, for all who may hereafter have to struggle for the restoration or extension of their rights. [But] her influence as well as her example, will be wanted in the crisis which seems to be approaching; and that influence must be paralyzed and inoperative, if she shall think [it] a duty to divide herself from England. . . .

A FRENCH INTELLECTUAL LOOKS TO AMERICA*

French intellectuals, from the eighteenth century on, have taken a deep interest in American life. They have often been critical of its lack of culture, its supposed standardization, and its alleged inadequacies in providing for the creative spirit. On the other hand many of France's intellectuals found much of value in America's example. Ernest Renan was among them when he reminded fellow Frenchmen of America's role in freeing the human mind.

⚹   ⚹   ⚹

The world is moving in the direction of what I may call a kind of Americanism, which shocks our refined ideas, but which, once the crisis of the present hour is over, may very possibly be less inimical than the *ancien régime* to the only thing of any real importance: viz. the emancipation and progress of the human mind. . . . The one object in life is the development of the mind, and the first condition for the development of the mind is that it should have liberty. The worst social state from this point of view is the theocratic state . . . in which dogma reigns supreme. . . . The belief or the opinion of the one side should not be a fetter upon the other side. . . .

This is a state of things which is coming to an end in our time, and we must not be surprised if some disturbance ensues. There are no longer masses who believe; a great number of the people decline to recognize the supernatural, and the day is not far distant when beliefs of this kind will die out altogether in the masses, just as the beliefs in familiar spirits and ghosts have disappeared. . . .

There can be no denying that it will take time for the

* Ernest Renan, *Recollections of My Youth*, translated from the French by C. B. Pitman and revised by Mme. Renan (London, 1883), pp. xiii-xxi.

liberty, which is the aim and object of human society, to take root in France as it has in America. . . .

I quite think that if democratic ideas were to secure a definitive triumph, science and scientific teaching would soon find the modest subsidies now accorded them cut off. This is an eventuality which would have to be accepted as philosophically as may be. . . . The plaudits and favour of the public will, for a long time to come, be at the service of what is false. But the true has great power, when it is free; the true endures; the false is ever changing and decays. Thus it is that the true, though only understood by a select few, always rises to the surface, and in the end prevails.

In short, it is very possible that the American-like social condition towards which we are advancing, independently of any particular form of government, will not be more intolerable for persons of intelligence than the better guaranteed social conditions which we have already been subject to. We may at least hope that vulgarity will not yet a while persecute freedom of mind. Descartes, living in the brilliant seventeenth century, was nowhere so well off as at Amsterdam, because, as "everyone was engaged in trade there," no one paid any heed to him. It may be that general vulgarity will one day be the condition of happiness, for the worst American vulgarity would not send Giordano Bruno to the stake or persecute Galileo. . . . We shall pass through several alternatives of anarchy and despotism before we find repose in this happy medium. But liberty is like truth; scarcely anyone loves it on its own account, and yet, owing to the impossibility of extremes, one always comes back to it.

CROSSCURRENTS IN EDUCATION*

Education, from the earliest years of the Atlantic Civilization, reveals the continual interplay between Europe and America. When Americans were wrestling with the problem of improving public education in the Jacksonian era they sent commissions to study Europe's education programs. These American visitors eventually published reports which were very influential among educators in their native land. (See E. W. Knight, ed., Reports on European Education, *New York, 1930.) When Europeans were debating educational policies, those advocating freedom from sectarian control sought support in American example. On higher levels of education, for a long time America was a heavy debtor to Europe, but eventually influences operated in both directions. The following selections illustrate these crosscurrents.*

✓ ✓ ✓

[*From Richard Cobden's American Diaries.*] July 10 [*1835*]—then we walk to see an infant school [in New England] pregnant with hopes of the exaltation of the character of future generations! I hereby dedicate myself to the task of promoting the cause of infant schools in England where they may become an instrument for ameliorating the fate of the children working in the factories whose case I fear is beyond the reach of all other remedies. . . .

[*To William Tait after visit to America.*] If you travel in that Country every man of whatever shade of politics will avow that his hopes of the permanency of sound democratic self-government, free from anarchy on the one hand and tyranny on the other, are based entirely

* E. H. Cawley, ed., *The American Diaries of Richard Cobden* (Princeton, 1952), pp. 26, 27, 28, 70, 71, 121. Reprinted by permission of Princeton University Press.

upon the great and increasing knowledge of the masses:
—education—education—education is the motto of every
enlightened democrat in America. . . .

[*From a speech at the National Public Schools' Association in Manchester.*] You must secure a law which, as
in the case of the New England States, as in the State of
Massachusetts, for instance, compels every locality or
parish to furnish a school and the means of education to
the whole of the people, and furnish not merely a building
such as our orders in council are now aiming at. . . .

[*To George Combe, November 9, 1850.*] I shall now go
straight at the mark, and shall neither give nor take
quarter—I have made up my mind to go for the Massachusetts system as nearly as we can get it. . . .

[*To Daniel Gilman, visiting American educator, requesting him to address a Manchester meeting, 1854.*] One difficulty is our religious question. Show the meeting how you
reconcile the rights of conscience on religious matters and
the demands of society for secular instruction. Give us
some statistics of what you are doing in the States and
shame us out of our intolerance and supineness. Tell the
meeting strongly that you consider in America that all
you possess that is most precious in social development
and political freedom you owe solely, under Providence,
to your system of education. . . .

Comparing what I now [1859] see with what I remember
of the America of 1835, the progress in material and
moral prosperity realizes all that I had expected to see.
The people are far better off to my eyes as compared with
the Europe of today than they were in 1835 as compared
with the old world at that time. What strikes me now
even more than it did then is the obviously higher grade
at which the social habits of the working class are pitched
as compared with the same class in the old country.

[*Mayor William Biggs, Leicester, England, speaks in
favor of National Education, reported in* Leicestershire
Mercury, *April 28, 1849.*] The plan contemplated the
establishment of a system like that of the United States,
not like that of Prussia. All rate payers were to elect a
local board, a commissioner of education, such board to
be empowered to lay rates (like boards of guardians),
build schools, appoint schoolmasters, etc. [*Biggs went on
to answer opponents who say government has no right*

to interfere with education of the people.] If in America where political rights were well understood and carefully cherished—where every man formed part of the nation, and was (so to speak) heir to the throne—if there it was thought right to delegate these educational powers to Government, the Government had a right to exercise them derived from the most legitimate source. (*Hear.*) In a free country, the words government and society ought to be synonymous terms: what the latter could do, could be done by the former, which was but society reduced in a scale of numbers. (*Hear.*) [Americans do better than Canadians and our other colonies. In the United States with its sectarian rivalries, a] national and unsectarian system of education was adopted with great success . . . surely if opposed sects could thus agree in the New England states, we ought to be able to do the same in this Old Anglo-Saxon land of ours. (*Applause.*) [*The Mayor then read communications from America showing how well unsectarian plan worked there, American bounty to education, etc., and then concluded:*] We hope to see the day when the term *Charity School* shall have become obsolete (*Hear, hear*) and when Public Schools shall be provided, to which a man will have no more feeling of degradation in sending his children than he now has in using a high road provided in like manner at the common expense. (*Loud cheers.*)

[*European countries sent commissions to study American educational practice, M. Siljestrom (Sweden), Rev. James Fraser (England), and M. C. Hippeau (France). All published reports. Fraser's, in 1867, urged England to adopt the American system of graded schools; he remarked:*] Americans, if not the most highly educated, are certainly the most generally educated and intelligent people on the earth.

[*Hippeau's report,* L'Instruction Publique aux Etats-Unis, *was published in 1870.*] If the spirit of initiative, which seems at the moment I write these lines, to be awakened among us, can find encouragement in the picture of great deeds being accomplished in America, it would be the sweetest recompense that I can derive from my trip and from the book in which I have described its results. [American youngsters arrived at college age in the best condition to make rapid progress:] They are not, as are the students of our lycées, fatigued and wasted by six or seven years devoted to the study of Latin and Greek grammar, to the composition of themes and to Latin verse. [While American colleges cannot yet compare with great European universities, their immense resources and their will not to be surpassed promise for them a rich future.]

[*What follows are some of Hippeau's observations in paraphrase.*] Physical education was important in America; it would be difficult to tell the children of the poor from the children of the rich. Primary school in the United States is a first link between the different classes of society, while the primary school in Europe established and consecrates the point of departure for inequality and the separation of classes. American classroom techniques were often admirable, stimulating the spirit of observation, reflection, and reasoning. While Europe still discusses the question as to the extent of schooling to be made available to women and whether they were capable of advanced education, one country long since resolved that question, the United States. Among the faults in American education was the insufficient stimulus to the imagination; history was too often a collection of facts. To avoid the terrible effects of ignorance and social disorder, France should emulate the American system of public education.

[*Americans were long discontented with their deficiencies in higher education. Daniel C. Gilman, first president of Johns Hopkins, was one who did much to remedy these deficiencies. Another, was his friend, Andrew D. White, professor of history at Michigan, then first president of Cornell. Both men studied abroad. The following comes from the* Autobiography of Andrew Dickson White.*]

The historical works of Buckle, Lecky, and Draper, which were then appearing, gave me a new and fruitful impulse; but most stimulating of all was the atmosphere coming from the great thought of Darwin and Herbert Spencer—an atmosphere in which history became less and less a matter of annals, and more and more a record of the unfolding of humanity. . . . My favorite studies at Yale had been history and kindred subjects, but these had been taught mainly from text-books. Lectures were

* From Andrew Dickson White, *Autobiography* (New York, 1914). Printed by permission of the publishers, Appleton-Century-Crofts, Inc.

few and dry. . . . But men like Arnould, St. Marc Girardin, and Laboulaye in France, and Lepsius, Ritter, Von Raumer, and Curtius in Germany, lecturing to large bodies of attentive students on the most interesting and instructive periods of human history, aroused in me a new current of ideas. Gradually I began to ask myself the question: Why not help the beginnings of this system in the United States. . . . In these great foreign universities, one means of making a reform became evident . . . the substitution of lectures for recitations, and the creation of an interest in history by treating it as living subject having relations to present questions. . . .

In order that my work might be fairly well based, I had, during my college days and my first stay abroad, begun collecting [a] private library [of original materials]. I found that passages actually read from important originals during my lectures gave a reality and vividness to my instruction which were otherwise unattainable. A citation of the very words themselves [used by] Erasmus, or Luther . . . or Robespierre, or Marat, interested my students far more than any quotation at second hand could do. . . . In this way alone can history be made real to students. . . .

[American universities, the best of them, long since became the peers of European schools, and in the twentieth century have surpassed them in many respects. American mathematicians deeply impressed young English scholars, who thought that only in Cambridge and possibly Manchester were their equals to be found.] Mathematicians in Europe are only beginning to realize the tremendous strides the subject has made in America—it is time they did, for in this as in so many other fields of activity, she is becoming the leader of the world. [See S. Gorley Putt, ed., *Cousins and Strangers: Comments on America by Commonwealth Fund Fellows from Britain, 1946-1952* (Cambridge, Mass., 1956), p. 112.]

MIXED REACTION OF AMERICANS TO ENGLAND *

Americans, particularly in the period between the War of 1812 and the Civil War, were frequently torn between two emotions in their attitude to England. On the one hand, there was affection for the old Mother country with pride in a common cultural heritage. On the other hand, there was resentment against real and fancied snubs by English critics of New World society. Hawthorne expresses this mixture of sentiments in Our Old Home, *based on his stay in Liverpool as consul.*

✓   ✓   ✓

While an American willingly accepts growth and change as the law of his own national and private existence, he has a singular tenderness for the stone-incrusted institutions of the mother-country. The reason may be . . . that he recognizes the tendency of these hardened forms to stiffen her joints and fetter her ankles, in the race and rivalry of improvement. I hated to see so much as a twig of ivy wrenched away from an old wall in England. Yet change is at work. . . .

An American is not very apt to love the English people, as a whole, on whatever length of acquaintance. I fancy that they would value our regard, and even reciprocate it in their ungracious way, if we could give it to them in spite of all rebuffs; but they are beset by a curious and inevitable infelicity, which compels them, as it were, to keep up what they seem to consider a wholesome bitterness of feeling between themselves and all other nationalities, especially that of America. They will never confess it; nevertheless, it is as essential a tonic to them as their bitter ale. Therefore—and possibly, too, from a similar

* Nathaniel Hawthorne, *Our Old Home and English Note-Books* (Boston, 1883), Vol. I, pp. 79, 83-84.

narrowness in his own character,—an American seldom feels quite as if he were at home among the English people. If he do so, he has ceased to be an American. But it requires no long residence to make him love their island, and appreciate it as thoroughly as they themselves do. For my part, I used to wish that we could annex it, transferring their thirty millions of inhabitants to some convenient wilderness in the great West, and putting half or a quarter as many of ourselves into their places. The change would be beneficial to both parties. We, in our dry atmosphere, are getting too nervous, haggard, dyspeptic, extenuated, unsubstantial, theoretic, and need to be made grosser. John Bull, on the other hand, has grown bulbous, long-bodied, short-legged, heavy-witted, material, and, in a word, too intensely English. In a few more centuries he will be the earthliest creature that ever the earth saw. Heretofore Providence has obviated such a result by timely intermixtures of alien races with the old English stock; so that each successive conquest of England has proved a victory by the revivification and improvement of its native manhood. Cannot America and England hit upon some scheme to secure even greater advantages to both nations?

— Reading No. 20 —

TRANSATLANTIC HUMANITARIANISM*

European liberals usually pointed to American example as worthy of emulation in alleviating human misery and

* A. H. Abel and F. J. Klingberg, *A Side-light on Anglo-American Relations, 1839-1858* (Lancaster, Pa., 1927), pp. 13-14, 55, 140, 195, 296, 308, 319. Printed by permission of the Association for the Study of Negro Life and History, Inc.

indignity. But Americans reversed the tribute on occasion, especially with respect to the abolition of slavery.

✓   ✓   ✓

The venerable [Thomas] Clarkson still lives, we rejoice to learn, and employs his active pen in the good cause. He is held in grateful remembrance here [America] by those who have seen his revered face & by the tens of thousands who have perused his works. May his last days be his best days. [*Tappan to Beaumont, Jan. 30, 1844.*]

The abolition of slavery in the Colonies of Great Britain . . . was an event, at which, if the whole human race could have been concentrated in one person, the heart of that person would have leaped for joy. The restoration of eight hundred thousand human beings from a state of grinding oppression to the rights bestowed upon them by the God of nature at their birth, was of itself a cause of rejoicing to the pure in heart throughout the habitable earth. But that is not the only nor the most radiant glory of that day. It was the pledge of power and of will of the mightiest nation upon the globe, that the bondage of man shall cease . . . that the self-evident truths of our Declaration of Independence shall no longer be idle mockeries. . . . [*John Quincy Adams to Anna Q. Thaxter, July 29, 1844.*]

It would be well if more powerful articles could be published in your [British] Quarterlies of which 2000 copies are regularly printed and circulated in the United States. The facts in regard to Slavery and the Slave Trade, the true results of West India Emancipation . . . would thus find a place in every public Library and brought fully before the most intelligent and reading minds, in all parts of the country, South as well as North. [*Leavitt to Sturge, New York, July 5, 1839.*]

It is very gratifying to the friends of freedom, as it is extremely annoying to our secular and religious pro-slavery papers, to hear of the immense sale of this work [*Uncle Tom's Cabin*] in England and other European countries, and the extraordinary interest the work excites. The citadel of Human Slavery is at length invested by a woman, whose missiles are doing execution on an unprecedented scale. [*Tappan to Bolton, Dec. 10, 1852.*]

At last the whole world is talking or reading about

American Slavery. The popularity of *Uncle Tom's Cabin*
and *The White Slave* [by Richard Hildreth] have com-
pelled the Booksellers to advertise them. And the many
pro-slavery pamphlets, got up on the emergency, to divert
public attention from the great works alluded to, have
utterly failed to effect that object. [*Tappan to British and
Foreign Anti-Slave Reporter, Feb. 15, 1853.*]

— Reading No. 21 —

EUROPEAN LIBERALS FAVOR THE NORTH IN THE CIVIL WAR*

*One of the most articulate of British liberals, Goldwin
Smith, came to Boston in 1864 to express the sympathy
of his group for the Northern cause. At the same time he,
like others before him, emphasized the need for Anglo-
Saxon solidarity against the threat of despotism.*

Let England and America quarrel, let your weight be
cast into the scale against us, when we struggle with the
great conspiracy of absolutist powers around us, and the
hope of freedom in Europe would be almost quenched.
. . . English liberties, imperfect as they may be . . .
are the source from which your liberties have flowed,
though the river may be more abundant than the spring.
Being in America, I am in England,—not only because
American hospitality makes me feel that I am still in my
own country, but because our institutions are fundamen-

* Goldwin Smith, *England and America*. Reprinted from the
    Atlantic Monthly, Vol. XIV, December, 1864 (Manchester,
    1865), pp. 4-22.

tally the same. The great foundations of constitutional government, legislative assemblies, parliamentary representation, personal liberty, self-taxation, the freedom of the press, allegiance to the law as a power above individual will,—all these were established . . . in the land from which the fathers of your republic came. . . . She [England] it was, that, having advanced by centuries of effort to the front of the Old World, became worthy to give birth to the New. From England you are sprung; and it is because you are Englishmen that English freedom, not French or Spanish despotism, is the law of this continent. From England you are sprung; and if the choice were given you among all the nations of the world, which would you rather choose for a mother?

In England the party of Cromwell and Milton still lives . . . and in this crisis of your fortunes, its heart turns to you. On your success ours depends. . . . An English Liberal comes here, not only to watch the unfolding of your destiny but to read his own. . . . The present Civil War is a vast episode in the same irrepressible conflict between Aristocracy and Democracy; and the heirs of the Cavalier in England sympathise with your enemies, the heirs of the Puritan with you. . . . [You can revenge yourselves in America upon the English aristocracy.] Succeed in your great experiment . . . the progress of opinion in England will in time do the rest. . . . If you are a standing menace to aristocracies, you are equally a standing menace to State Churches . . .

The England of Charles and Laud has been against you; the England of Hampden, Milton and Cromwell, has in the main been on your side.

EMIGRATION AND THE IMAGE OF AMERICA IN EUROPE*

Emigration from Europe to America is a central theme in the Atlantic Civilization. The fundamental factors that propelled millions across the sea were much the same in all countries, though there were special considerations in each community. One of the best students of emigration is Theodore C. Blegen, who has devoted many years to the study of Norwegian migration.

✓ ✓ ✓

Two peasants from Numedal, Ole and Ansten Nattestad, visited Stavanger in 1836 and there, apparently for the first time in their lives, "heard much talk about a country which was called America." "We saw letters," writes Ole Nattestad, "written by Norwegians who were living in America and we were told that Knud Slogvig, who many years before that had emigrated in a sloop from Stavanger, had lately visited his native land and had given so favorable a report about America that about 150 emigrants from Stavanger *Amt* and from Hardanger had gone back with him and had sailed that very summer in two brigs across the ocean. They had gone in spite of all sorts of threats and warnings about slavery, death, and disease." The two brothers had much to think of as they made their way back home to Numedal. Their father, Knud Nattestad, owned a *gaard* or farm, which by right of primogeniture would go to their older brother. While the latter was away at a military school, Ole had been given the management of the farm. He found at the end of a year that he had little or nothing left as a reward for his labor, and he

* Theodore C. Blegen, *Norwegian Migration to America, 1825-1860* (Northfield, Minn., 1931), pp. 85-86, 166-167, 318, 342, 343-344. Reprinted by permission of The Norwegian-American Historical Association.

decided that it would be useless to buy a farm and go into debt. He then became an itinerant trader, but because of restrictive laws was forced to abandon this occupation. He then worked for a time as a blacksmith. Thereupon, with his brother, he made the trip to Stavanger. The following Christmas he visited a prominent man of the community, a member of the Storthing, and discussed with him the economic conditions of the valley, asking him for advice. This man, Even Nubbru, replied that wherever he went in the world, he would nowhere find a people who had as good laws as the Americans. "This information," says Ole Nattestad, "had a magic effect on me, as I looked upon it as an injustice that the laws of Norway should forbid me to trade and not allow me to get my living by honest work as a mechanic wherever I desired to settle. I had confidence in the judgment of a member of the Storthing and I compared his remarks with what I had heard about America in the vicinity of Stavanger. Gradually I got to thinking of emigration while considering the matter on my way home, and the idea matured into a resolution. My brother Ansten did not have to be asked a second time. . . ."

The emigrants themselves, in explaining their action, emphasize the economic difficulties in Norway and the hope of winning a better livelihood in America, but they frequently touch also on social, political, and religious issues. [Johan R.] Reiersen in 1843, after visiting many Norwegian immigrants in the West and inquiring about their motives for emigrating, drew up a list of particulars. . . .

1. The gloomy prospects in Norway for the future of the rising generation, coupled with the hope of independence and happiness in America.

2. The fact that for the "producing and working class," Norway is too circumscribed; that there is not room enough; and that the time is not distant when "a slavish dependence" will become general.

3. General dissatisfaction with the administration of Norwegian law, especially with reference to relations between debtors and creditors, where the regulations in force work the ruin of the former.

4. A general feeling that the state does too little to promote agriculture and the welfare of the common

people, though it devotes large sums of money to other purposes.

5. Dissatisfaction with Norwegian officialdom and the clergy, which form a caste that looks upon an ordinary citizen as an inferior.

6. Failure in Norway to realize the freedom and equality that the constitution of 1814 promised.

7. The pressure . . . of poor-relief burdens.

8. The pressure . . . of burdens connected with the Norwegian road system.

9. Uncertainty of crops and sterility of the soil.

10. Idealization of America. . . .

[Adolph] Tidemand [a Norwegian painter] picturing a farewell scene inspired several poems, including [this] one:

> A fever sweeps over Norway's mountains into the most distant and hidden valleys. With fearful effect it seizes men and women; it carries people off by the thousands. From home and fireside the younger generation depart—and the aged sorrow in lonely huts.
>
> To the West! To America! Thus comes the mighty call from over the western sea. And in response great throngs set forth to another home—or to an early grave. Has the Fatherland nothing wherewith to feed its own children, since they thus desert it?
>
> Ah, yes! Poor indeed old Norway may be, but it has ever bread to reward industrious toil. And for its mountain homes it has the shelter of freedom. And it has the sweet speech of the motherland. Still, those caught in the toils of the fever must go! Alas, neither wise counsel nor upbraiding is of any avail. . . .

The advertising of the West proceeded vigorously in the fifties. . . . And there were also some novel types of "America advertising." In the summer of 1852, for example, a panorama of the Mississippi River and valley was exhibited for some six weeks in Christiania. Such exhibits, made up of great unwinding rolls of canvas with successions of painted scenes, were the motion pictures of the fifties; and then—as now with the cinema—representations of the wild West were very popular in Europe. Unwound to the accompaniment of a lecture, the one shown in Christiania—it was reported to contain sixty thousand square feet of canvas—pictured America's great

river from the Falls of St. Anthony to the Gulf. A newspaper reviewer predicted that it would not be long before
those falls would be harnessed, the nucleus of factories
and a great city. Thus the future Minneapolis was hailed
in Norway before the Norwegian immigrants themselves
fully understood the prospects of Minnesota. A. O. Vinje,
the well known Norwegian poet, saw the Mississippi
panorama and got from it a new understanding of American strenuosity. America, he believed, was destined to
conquer the whole world. . . .

Fredrika Bremer's *Homes of the New World* . . . was
undoubtedly an influential and widely read work in all
the Scandinavian countries, as it was in England and the
United States. The Swedish novelist's prophetic rhapsody
after viewing the upper Northwest is famous: "What a
glorious new Scandinavia might not Minnesota become!
Here would the Swede find again his clear, romantic
lakes; . . . here would the Norwegian find his rapid
rivers . . . and both nations their hunting fields and
their fisheries. The Danes might here pasture their flocks
and herds, and lay out their farms on richer and less misty
coasts than those of Denmark. . . . The climate, the
situation, the character of the scenery, agrees with our
people better than that of any other of the American
States. . . .

— Reading No. 23 —

MELVILLE DESCRIBES GERMAN EMIGRANTS TO AMERICA*

*Herman Melville as a young man spent a few weeks in
Liverpool, where he saw emigrants embarking for Amer-*

* Herman Melville, *Redburn,* Chapter XXXIII.

*ica. He was touched by their hopes, and he was moved
to write in* Redburn *a noble statement of the meaning of
America for humanity.*

✓   ✓   ✓

There was hardly anything I witnessed in the docks that
interested me more than the German emigrants who come
on board the large New York ships several days before
their sailing, to make everything comfortable ere starting.
Old men, tottering with age, and little infants in arms;
laughing girls in bright-buttoned bodices, and astute,
middle-aged men with pictured pipes in their mouths,
would be seen mingling together in crowds of five, six and
seven or eight hundred in one ship.

Every evening these countrymen of Luther and Me-
lancthon gathered on the forecastle to sing and pray. And
it was exalting to listen to their fine ringing anthems,
reverberating among the crowded shipping, and rebound-
ing from the lofty walls of the docks. Shut your eyes, and
you would think you were in a cathedral.

They keep up this custom at sea; and every night, in
the dogwatch, sing the songs of Zion to the roll of the
great ocean-organ: a pious custom of a devout race, who
thus send over their hallelujahs before them, as they hie
to the land of the stranger.

And among these sober Germans, my country counts
the most orderly and valuable of her foreign population.
It is they who have swelled the census of her North-
western States; and transferring their ploughs from the hills
of Transylvania to the prairies of Wisconsin; and sowing
the wheat of the Rhine on the banks of the Ohio, raise
the grain, that, a hundred fold increased, may return to
their kinsmen in Europe.

There is something in the contemplation of the mode
in which America has been settled, that, in a noble breast,
should forever extinguish the prejudices of national dislikes.

Settled by the people of all nations, all nations may
claim her for their own. You can not spill a drop of
American blood without spilling the blood of the whole
world. . . . We are not a narrow tribe of men. . . . No:
our blood is as the flood of the Amazon, made up of a
thousand noble currents all pouring into one. We are

not a nation, so much as a world. . . . We are the heirs of all time, and with all nations we divide our inheritance. On this Western Hemisphere all tribes and people are forming into one federated whole; and there is a future which shall see the estranged children of Adam restored as to the old hearth-stone in Eden. . . .

— Reading No. 24 —

EFFECTS OF EMIGRATION UPON EUROPE*

The continued drain of Europe's most virile blood caused the Old World to think of ways to stanch the flow. Sweden, in particular, suffered depletion in the later half of the nineteenth century, causing her much soul-searching. Professor Franklin D. Scott has made a close study of the impact of emigration upon Sweden, whose problems resembled those faced by other countries.

⟡   ⟡   ⟡

By the early 1900's the nation [Sweden] was roused to action on the anti-emigration front. In 1904 C. J. Jacobson introduced in the *riksdag* a resolution calling for a thorough investigation of the causes of emigration and of possible means of curbing it, and prefaced the motion with an estimate of the situation: ". . . annually several thousand vigorous young persons leave the fatherland to seek in a foreign country a living which with industry and saving they could as well attain here at home, and more would do so if they realized the hardships that most go forth to meet in a strange land. . . . Information on

* F. D. Scott, *The Causes and Consequences of Emigration in Sweden.* Reprinted by permission from *The Chronicle* (Spring, 1955), published by the American Swedish Historical Foundation, Philadelphia.

the dangers of emigration would in large degree check the stream. . . . Another method of checking emigration is to provide a better future for youth here at home. Workers can be given more pleasant work and better wages here than in most places abroad. . . . It is the prospect of securing one's own home that drives hordes of Swedish men and women to America. But the opportunity to own a home can be provided better in Sweden than elsewhere. . . . (This requires state assistance with draining marshes, parceling the land, and granting loans on reasonable conditions.) This would be the best protection against emigration to America. There was a time, happily long past, when need prevailed in the country, when people were impoverished by bad years and unwise financial policy. . . . Now the times are different . . . and Sweden can give shelter and bread to its sons and daughters, and also to those who have forsaken the fatherland but wish to return. . . ."

A month later Ernst Beckman produced a similar memoir, well-reasoned, and deploring that Sweden should "with hands in pocket, quiet and inactive, watch this 'bloodletting of the Swedish nation.'" He sounded the positive note of reform: an own-home movement, universal suffrage, widened education, tax reform, and improved economic opportunity "would without doubt help to control or diminish emigration." Therefore the state should sponsor a social-statistical survey of emigration . . . an investigation of what steps to take to promote re-immigration of the emigrated; . . . and a study of "American conditions especially economy and popular education, in order to discover what might be worthy of imitation." . . . Beckman emphasized the value to Sweden of the "practical experience and the new ideas obtained by the emigrated during their learning years in America [which] would have an awakening and spurring effect in the community where they resettled." The study, he said, should "absorb all the really good to be found in America in order, to use a well-known phrase, 'to move America over to Sweden' and so to bring our youth to see their own country as the 'land of the future.'" The question was vital for all Europe: "why America in industry and several other areas can offer workers such favorable terms, and what the reason is for its superiority . . . which has brought it about that in much America has become the teacher of the Old World." . . . [Beckman] praised the broad general education in the United States, the free public libraries, the "magnificent information on the agricultural question in several states," and the experimental farms.

At length the great investigation was approved, and work began in . . . 1907. . . . The best presentation of grievances came from the emigrants themselves. . . . More dramatic than the interviews were the letters to the commission from earlier emigrants settled in America. One had emigrated in 1868, twice returned to Sweden with his savings, but finally settled in America. His reasoning was primarily economic, but his long letter closed with a bitter and revealing comparison: "Here [in America] we have rich men, here we have learned men, here we have 'clever' men, here we have workbosses who sometimes browbeat us—but *masters* (*herrar*) we do not have." Another closed . . . with advice to Mother Svea: "When you give your children universal suffrage (for it is at the ballot box that class differences vanish), when you separate church and state, when you modernize some of your antique laws and take education away from the priesthood, then I shall sell all that I have here [in America] and go home to rest in your earth." . . .

What . . . [were] the effects of emigration on Sweden? The most persistent grievance of the emigrants was their inability to acquire homes for themselves in Sweden, and this led to an attempt to develop a Swedish frontier, to substitute home-building in Lappland for adventure on the Great Plains. In 1899 a proposal was made in the *riksdag* for state aid to home-seekers; in 1904 legislation provided for state-financed low-interest loans to homebuilders. As one of the promoters of this act remarked . . . its purpose was to "establish homes . . . strengthen the economic position of the less well-off, counteract emigration, and promote cultivation of the land." . . .

The National Society against Emigration, founded in 1907 and aided by the state, published books on housing and settlement in the United States and Canada, studies of work intensity in Sweden and America, and brochures on social and economic problems directly aimed at checking emigration by reforming conditions in Sweden. . . .

In the ensuing years, more and more Swedes could and did own their own farms—over 90% of Swedish farms were owned by their operators in 1950. . . .

The evidence is clear that [emigration] was a force contributing to the program of land reclamation and settlement, to the democratization of educational opportunity and the extension of practical education, to the expansion of the suffrage and the leveling of class distinctions, to the rationalization of industry, and to the development of shipping (especially the founding of the Swedish-American Line). Indirectly emigration influenced the establishment of a state mortgage bank (1909) and the study of old age insurance leading to the pension act of 1913. . . .

Tangible enough were the emigrant remittances. That part which came in postal money orders amounted to about $100,000,000 between 1885 and 1937. Swedish estimates of total remittances between 1906 and 1930 put them at eight to ten million dollars per year. To many a struggling family their share of these free gifts meant an important plus in income, the comforts of life, or new machinery. For the country this represented 0.4% of gross national income; in terms of the balance of payments with foreign countries it was 25% in the decade of the 1920s.

Emigrants had a profound effect on the free church movement and religious toleration. It was recognized that emigration was most appealing to the same social classes in which religious dissent flourished, and the exodus of the Eric Janssonists in the 1840s made a deep impression. . . . The restrictive Conventicle Act was repealed in 1860. Still more significant as a continuing influence was the steady travel back and forth between Sweden and America of a number . . . who preached the personal religious faith of the Methodists, the Baptists, and the Mission Covenanters. It was such people, too, who took the Good Templar Order from America to Sweden and did their best to win the Swedes to temperance. Out of the free churches came many of the later reforming political leaders. The demand for widened suffrage was stimulated by this religious emphasis on personality and human rights, and was reinforced by the appeal of full political rights in America. . . .

Prime minister of Sweden, Tage Erlander, speaking in 1952 in Minneapolis [said]: "It was once considered a tremendous loss to Sweden that more than one million Swedish men and women chose to leave their native country to find new opportunities on the other side of the Atlantic. Today, however, we realize that this loss has become an asset. It has laid the foundation for a deeper understanding between the United States and Sweden and stimulated the exchange of knowledge and experiences. Thanks to the Swedish immigrant, America became a living reality in almost every Swedish home and a challenge even to those who stayed in the old country, spurring them to seek new opportunities and to utilize modern American technique in order to raise their standard of living."

— Reading No. 25 —

THE VISION OF AMERICA IN ITALY*

The links between Italy and America grew close when Italians began emigrating to the New World in large numbers. America became a mixture of reality and myth to Old World Italians. Carlo Levi, the distinguished Italian novelist, captured this vision of his countrymen in the pages of his Christ Stopped at Eboli.

↗   ↗   ↗

The houses [in Gagliano, southern Italy] were nearly all of only one room, with no windows, drawing their light from the door. . . . Here and there was a house with a

* Carlo Levi, *Christ Stopped at Eboli* (New York, 1947), pp. 43, 102, 122, 123-124, 125-126, 127, 131-132. Reprinted by permission of the publishers, Farrar, Straus and Cudahy, Inc.

second story and a balcony, where the front door was not made of worn black wood, but had a conspicuous coat of shiny varnish and was decked out with a brass doorknob. Such houses belonged to the "Americans." . . .

Emigration has changed the picture. The men have gone and the women have taken over. Many a woman's husband is in America. For a year, or even two, he writes to her, then he drops out of her ken, perhaps he forms other family ties; in any case he disappears and never comes back. The wife waits for him a year, or even two; then some opportunity arises and a baby is the result. A great part of the children are illegitimate; and the mother holds absolute sway. Gagliano has twelve hundred inhabitants, and there are two thousand men from Gagliano in America. Grassano has five thousand inhabitants and almost the same number have emigrated. In the villages the women outnumber the men and the father's identity is no longer so strictly important; honor is dissociated from paternity, because a matriarchal regime prevails. . . .

What never failed to strike me most of all—and by now I had been in almost every house—were the eyes of the two inseparable guardian angels that looked at me from the wall over the bed. On one side was the black, scowling face, with its large, inhuman eyes, of the Madonna of Viggiano; on the other a colored print of the sparkling eyes, behind gleaming glasses, and the hearty grin of President Roosevelt. I never saw other pictures or images than these; not the King nor the Duce, nor even Garibaldi; no famous Italian of any kind, nor any one of the appropriate saints; only Roosevelt and the Madonna of Viggiano never failed to be present. To see them there, one facing the other, in cheap prints, they seemed the two faces of the power that had divided the universe between them. But here their roles were, quite rightly, reversed. The Madonna appeared to be a fierce, pitiless, mysterious, ancient earth goddess, the Saturnial mistress of this world; the President a sort of all-powerful Zeus, the benevolent and smiling master of a higher sphere. Sometimes a third image formed, along with these two, a trinity: a dollar bill, the last of those brought back from across the sea, or one that had come in the letter of a husband or relative, was tacked up under the Ma-

donna or the President, or else between them, like the
Holy Ghost or an ambassador from heaven to the world
of the dead. . . .

Their [the peasant's] other world is America. . . .
America, to the peasants, has a dual nature. It is a land
where a man goes to work, where he toils and sweats for
his daily bread, where he lays aside a little money only
at the cost of endless hardship and privation, where he
can die and no one will remember him. At the same time,
and with no contradiction in terms, it is an earthly
paradise and the promised land.

Yes, New York, rather than Rome or Naples, would
be the real capital of the peasants of Lucania, if these
men without a country could have a capital at all. And
it *is* their capital, in the only way it can be for them, that
is as a myth. As a place to work, it is indifferent to them;
they live there as they would live anywhere else, like
animals harnessed to a wagon, heedless of the street where
they must pull it. But as an earthly paradise, Jerusalem
the golden, it is so sacred as to be untouchable; a man can
only gaze at it, even when he is there on the spot, with no
hope of attainment. The peasants who emigrate to America
remain just what they always were; many stay there and
their children become Americans, but the rest, those who
come back twenty years later, are just the same as when
they went away. In three months they forget the few
words of English they ever learned, slough off the few
superficial new habits and are the same peasants they
were before. . . . In America they live apart, among
themselves; for years they eat nothing but bread, just
as they did in Gagliano, saving all their meager earnings.
They live next door to the earthly paradise, but they dare
not enter.

Then one day they come back to Italy, with the intention of staying only long enough to visit their family and
friends. But someone offers to sell them a parcel of land,
and they run into a girl whom they knew when they were
children and decide to marry her. Before they are aware
of it, six months have gone by, their re-entry permit has
expired, and they have to stay home. The land was sold
to them at an exorbitant price, and the savings of years
of hard work in America go to pay for it; it is a mass of
clay and rocks, they must pay taxes on it, and the harvest

never makes up for their expenses; . . . Soon they sink back into poverty . . . in short these "Americans" can in no way be distinguished from the rest, unless it be by deeper bitterness, and the regret that from time to time haunts them for their lost riches. Gagliano is full of these returned emigrants, who look on the day of their return as the unluckiest of their lives. . . .

There were three barber shops in Gagliano, and the "American's," at the upper end of the village, near the church and just below the widow's house, was the only one open all the time; it was patronized by the gentry. . . . [It] was the only one that looked like the real thing. There was a mirror clouded with fly-tracks, some straight chairs, and, on the walls, clippings from American newspapers with photographs of Roosevelt and other political leaders and screen actresses and advertisements for cosmetics. These were the remains of his sumptuous establishment in New York. When the barber thought of old times his face grew dark and sad. What was left to him of the life of ease he had led on the other side? A little house at the upper end of the village, with an elaborately carved door and geranium pots on the balcony . . . and poverty. "If only I hadn't come back!" You can tell these Americans . . . by their whipped-dog expression and their gold teeth. . . .

After the fateful year of 1929 few came back from New York and few went over. The villages of Lucania, with half their people on one side of the ocean and half on the other, were split in two. Families were broken up and many women were left alone. To those who were left behind, America seemed farther away than ever, and their every hope of salvation gone. Only the mail faithfully brought remembrances from overseas, gifts to their families from those blessed by fortune. Don Cosimino was kept busy with these packages; they sent a stream of scissors, knives, razors, farm tools, scythes, hammers, pincers—in short, all the gadgets of everyday use. Life at Gagliano was entirely American in regard to mechanical equipment as well as weights and measures, for the peasants spoke of pounds and inches rather than of kilograms and centimeters. The women wove on ancient looms, but they cut their thread with shiny scissors from Pittsburg; the barber's razor was the best I ever saw anywhere in Italy, and

the blue steel blades of the peasants' axes were American.
The peasants had no prejudice against these modern in-
struments, nor did they see any contradiction between
them and their ancient customs. They simply took gladly
whatever came to them from New York, just as they
would take gladly whatever might come from Rome. But
from Rome came nothing. Nothing had ever come but the
tax collector and speeches over the radio.

— Reading No. 26 —

NORTH ATLANTIC TRIANGLE*

*The United Kingdom and the United States are the main
pillars of the North Atlantic civilization. To their strength,
in economic power and political imaginativeness, has been
added in recent years that of Canada. The interplay of
these three communities has been thoughtfully surveyed in
an original study by Professor J. B. Brebner.*

⚡   ⚡   ⚡

The most remarkable early effect of Napoleon's wars
on Anglo-American relations was the abrupt elevation of
the British North American colonies from obscurity and
poverty to prominence and prosperity. Britain discovered
that she needed not only all the timber, lumber, and wheat
which they could produce, but all that they could attract
to their ports from the United States. . . . The declining
Maritimes sprang to vigorous life; Quebec and Montreal

* J. B. Brebner, *North Atlantic Triangle: The Interplay of
    Canada, The United States and Great Britain* (New Ha-
    ven, 1945), pp. 81, 106, 128-129, 159-160, 165, 179, 188,
    193, 196, 197, 221, 224, 225, 226, 241. Reprinted by
    permission of The Carnegie Endowment for International
    Peace.

became great timber ports; and everywhere shipbuilding expanded rapidly. . . . In 1807 an imperial statute permitted the entry to British colonial ports from the United States of a large variety of provisions, wood products, and naval stores, and not only did these flow in abundantly from New England, upper Vermont, and the Lakes states, but American lumbermen and farmers migrated to British regions where their chances were better than at home. . . .

During the ensuing years [after the War of 1812] probably the underlying reason for Canada's salvation lay in the improved relations between Great Britain and the United States. If British North America was vulnerable to land attack, the American seaboard was vulnerable to the British navy. Gradually purely economic considerations triumphed over the ancient politico-economic orthodoxies which were the support of British sea power. The United States had forced its reëntry into the British mercantile empire on almost equal terms. An industrialized Great Britain was on the brink of an entirely new kind of economic nationalism which should be keyed to commercial reciprocities and free trade. This must be achieved by a gradual process, but it would revolutionize Britain's relations, not only with her colonies, but with the United States. Perhaps, therefore, the real reasons for the termination of the great trial of strength between Britons and their American offspring, and the foundation of the basic understanding between them which has survived a century and a quarter of exacting strains, are to be found in the Anglo-American collaboration which produced the Monroe Doctrine of 1823. . . .

In spite of a flood of emigrants' handbooks or guides, and a lively controversial literature in Great Britain about emigration, a great proportion of the newcomers had very vague ideas of the lands to which they were bound. For those who had read them, Fenimore Cooper's romantic tales had a way of leaving more lasting impressions than sober, informative works, and any appreciation of the scale and character of North American geography was quite rare. Thus an Irishman with no love for British rule sought a grant of land "in upper Kennedy in North America," and a group of wistful Scots in northern Ohio who were longing for familiar British institutions, when

they were asked why they did not simply cross Lake Erie
to enjoy them, replied: "We didna ken the difference
between the two governments; at the time we came over
here, it was a' America to us." . . .

Long before the Civil War broke out, British America
had taken its stand on Negro slavery. By the beginning of
the nineteenth century, practically all Negroes in the
provinces had been freed because their owners could not
depend on the courts to recognize such property rights.
Nova Scotia had even anticipated the later Liberian experiment of American friends of the Negro by transporting to Sierra Leone about twelve hundred Negroes of the
Loyalist migration. By 1833, when the British Parliament
formally emancipated all the slaves in the colonies, the
British North American provinces . . . had become to
terrified American colored folk "the land that we Negroes
call rock and our land of promise." . . . *Uncle Tom's
Cabin* was a best seller in both English and French ver-
sions. . . . Before Lincoln's election and even after his
declaration that his "paramount object" was to save the
Union, British Americans generally, like the liberals and
working men and women in England, insisted on attaching
the great conflict to the moral issue of slavery. . . .

About 1865 the new United States began to exact from
Great Britain a grudging, but steadily growing, respect as
a world power. As Richard Cobden said of his country's
politicians: "The alteration of tune is very remarkable. It is
clear that the homage which was refused to justice and
humanity will be freely given to success." . . .

The North Americans who worked so hard from 1858
to 1866 for Canadian federation had the United States
as an inspiration and a warning while they dreamed and
planned to bridge the continent. What Americans had
done they felt they could do, and in their constitution
they would remedy the central defect of the American constitution which the Civil War had revealed. Their intention, declared the Canadian Governor, Lord Monck, in
1866, "was to constitute a strong central authority the
power of which should be supreme and pervading throughout the Union with provincial bodies of a completely sub-
ordinate and municipal character for the administration of
purely local affairs." . . .

[Secretary of State Hamilton] Fish had been encouraged

to press forward toward his goal [settling the Alabama claims] because of his intimate understanding with the British Minister, Thornton. Great Britain had recently been rendered more amenable by the threats to her position in the world which were embodied in the Franco-Prussian War and in Russia's unilateral denunciation of the Black Sea neutrality provisions which had been imposed upon her at the end of the Crimean War. Gladstone's first reform ministry . . . was almost ready to acknowledge Great Britain's fault in the Civil War in order to foster Anglo-American friendship. . . . John Bassett Moore . . . in writing about the Treaty [of Washington, 1871] . . . placed it second in importance only to the Treaty of 1783 in American history, and said: "It was the greatest treaty of actual and immediate arbitration the world has ever seen. . . ."

Discouraging bickerings could only temporarily obscure what time has revealed to be the great and enduring achievements of 1871 at Washington. Of these unquestionably the greatest was the acceptance of the United States as a major Power by Great Britain and the laying of the foundations of an Anglo-American understanding which was based on substantial mutual respect. There were even some glimmerings of what was to prove to be a common outlook on world politics. . . . Anglo-American understanding was henceforth to be, if not always acknowledged, the cardinal principle of Canadian foreign policy, for if Great Britain and the United States began to pull in opposite directions the vulnerable Dominion of Canada was bound to be the first casualty. . . .

The twenty-five years following 1873 were probably the grimmest quarter century in the history of Canada. . . . The average Canadian standard of living during this period fell below the average in the United States, and, since there were no barriers to migration, many "surplus" Canadians . . . [moved] across the boundary. . . . Immigrants were pouring into Canada after 1851 in hundreds of thousands, but . . . after 1861 they were pouring out again into the United States about as fast as they entered. In addition, what had hitherto been a relatively minor outward seepage of native Canadians became a real torrent some time in the 'seventies. This combined emigration of immigrants and native Canadians for the *decade*

1881-1891 exceeded one million persons at a time when the total population of Canada was less than five millions. By 1895 the situation was so bad that had it continued Canada's population would speedily have become stationary. . . .

During [the] expansive quarter century (1896-1920), the economic triangle of buying and selling, investing and dividend-paying, migration and production, into which Great Britain, the United States, and Canada poured their efforts, became the mightiest thing of its kind on earth and seemed destined to remain so. . . . The three areas proved to be complementary in so many ways that they cooperated in spite of themselves.

Interestingly enough this economic cooperation persisted in spite of a curious procession of changes in the economic activity of the members. The United States rapidly assumed and expanded many of the industrial functions which Great Britain had once performed for her and for other parts of the world, and Canada, in a kind of breathless haste, not only took over much of the former American role of pouring forth raw and semi-manufactured products for the world market, but became increasingly capable in highly specialized industry. . . .

The restless peoples of Europe and North America dramatized the boom of 1896-1914 by their mass movements across the Atlantic and within the North American continent. The twin streams of humanity which entered the mouths of the St. Lawrence and the Hudson were the greatest in history. In North America two magnets of profitable enterprise, one west and one east, set up a clockwise international migration which deposited over a million Americans on the Canadian prairies and about a quarter of that number of Canadians in the industrial northeast of the United States. By these movements the population of Canada . . . grew faster than that of the United States. . . .

Canada and the United States conducted an almost continuous tariff war from 1865 to 1935 and yet trade between them grew until it was the largest exchange between two nations in the world. What was the explanation of this anomaly? Basically, of course, it meant that for the sake of maintaining a separate nationality Canadians were willing to pay higher prices for some goods, that is,

accept a slightly lower standard of living than that of the
United States, but since the latter was so far above any
European national standard, perhaps that did not matter
very much. Far more significant was the fact that eco-
nomically the two countries were Siamese twins who could
not live without each other. In facing the world they
might be rivals, but in relation to each other they were
complementary. . . .

— Reading No. 27 —

DISENCHANTMENT AND MATURITY*

*The traditional denigration by American intellectuals
and artists of their own country came to an end with the
depression of 1929 and disillusion with Europe. The
exiles returned with the belief that opportunities for the
creative individual would be as numerous in America as
in Europe. Disenchantment with the Old World was succeeded by more mature understanding of the New, and
ultimately of both.*

Everywhere, after the War, [1918] one found unfavorable comparisons between the intellectual life of America
and that of Europe. The critics often called for a great
American novel or opera; they were doggedly enthusiastic,
like cheer leaders urging Princeton to carry the ball over
the line; but at heart they felt that Princeton was beaten,
the game was in the bag for Oxford and the Sorbonne; at
heart they were not convinced that even the subject matter
of a great novel could be supplied by this country. Ameri-

* Malcolm Cowley, *Exile's Return* (New York, 1934), pp.
104-107. Reprinted by permission of The Viking Press Inc.

can themes were lacking in dignity. Art and ideas were products manufactured under a European patent; all we could furnish toward them was raw talent, destined usually to be wasted. Everywhere, in every department of cultural life, Europe offered the models to imitate—in painting, composing, philosophy, folk music, folk drinking, the drama, sex, politics. . . . As for our contemporary literature, thousands were willing to echo Van Wyck Brooks when he said that in comparison with the literature of any European country, 'it is indeed one long list of spiritual casualties. For it is not that the talent is wanting, but that somehow this talent fails to fulfill itself.'

Ten years later this feeling had gone and even its memory was fading. American intellectuals still complained, but their enemy was no longer 'civilization in the United States'; it was 'our business civilization,' it was efficiency, standardization, mass production, the machine —it was something that dominated our nation more than others, but affected the others also. Germany had yielded to it, Britain was yielding, even France was being poisoned —it was no use fleeing to London or Paris, though perhaps there was a secure village in the South of France, perhaps there was safety in Majorca. . . . People said that it was impossible to live in the United States, but not that it was impossible to write or paint there. Comparisons with European literature continued to be drawn, but not so often or so unfavorably. . . .

Something had changed, and the exiles of the 1920's had played their part in changing it. They had produced no Dostoyevsky, but for this simpler task no genius was required; they had merely to travel, compare, evaluate, and honestly record what they saw. In the midst of this process the burden of inferiority somehow disappeared— it was not so much dropped as it leaked away like sand from a bag carried on the shoulder—suddenly it was gone and nobody noticed the difference. Nobody even felt the need for inventing an American god, a myth to replace that of the business man; instead the exiles invented the international myth of the Lost Generation.

These young Americans had begun by discovering a crazy Europe in which the intellectuals of their own middle class were more defeated and demoralized than those at home. Later, after discounting the effects of the

War, they decided that all nations were fairly equal, some excelling in one quality, some in another—the Germans in mechanical efficiency, the French in self-assurance, the English in political acumen; the Americans excelled in wealth, but in most qualities they ranked midway in the scale: they were simply a nation among the other capitalist West European nations. Having registered this impression, the exiles were ready to find that their own nation had every attribute they had been taught to admire in those of Europe. It had developed its national types— who could fail to recognize an American in a crowd?—it possessed a folklore, and traditions, and the songs that embodied them; it had even produced new forms of art which the Europeans were glad to borrow. The exiles were preparing to embark on a voyage of discovery. Standing as it were on the Tour Eiffel, they looked southwestward across the wheatfields of Beauce and the rain-drenched little hills of Brittany, until somewhere in the mist they saw the country of their childhood, which should henceforth be the country of their art. American themes, like other themes, had exactly the dignity that talent could lend them. . . .

— Reading No. 28 —

EUROPE, A "FRONTIER" FOR AMERICANS*

Ever since Frederick Jackson Turner wrote his classic essay on the significance of the frontier in American history, students have been aware of the role of the West

* Philip Rahv, *Discovery of Europe: The Story of American Experience in the Old World* (Boston, 1947), pp. 417, 420, 421. Reprinted by permission of the publisher, Houghton Mifflin Company.

in the United States. In the history of America's intellec-
tual and artistic life there has been another frontier, the
Old World. From it has come a constant reinvigoration of
the life of the spirit. For a long time the ties were closest
with England, but eventually more and more Americans
found their deepest needs better satisfied by contact with
the Continent. Randolph Bourne was one such American
on the eve of the First World War.

↗   ↗   ↗

[*To Mary Messer, Paris, December 28, 1913.*]

Paris is a great spiritual relief after London, in whose atmosphere I began to feel suffocated. The impersonality, the deeply ingrained caste-system, the incorrigible moral optimism, the unproductive intellectualism, the lack of emotion or sensuousness, the barbarity of the outer aspects of English living, the insensitiveness to art, the insularity of ideas,—all exasperated my feelings and bumped against my ideas at every turn. Paris, democratic, artistic, social, sensuous, beautiful, represents almost the complete reversal of everything English. And the French writing, so personal, and so human; intellectualistic, but with concepts that light up vistas of experience and do not confuse them, as most English thought does. The irony and vivacity of the French temperament delight me; their total absence in England made it seem the most alien of all the countries I had seen.

[*To Alyse Gregory, Paris, March 18, 1914.*]

They [the French] are much more intellectually honest than the Anglo-Saxon. . . . My American friends soon weary of an argument, or insist on making it a personal matter, with slightly ruffled feelings on both sides. . . . The French are incomparable social psychologists in everything they write. It is a sense that we sadly lack. . . . The fact is, we Americans have the most incorrigible obstinacy to seeing things as they are, to looking facts in the face. We hystericalize, sentimentalize, and moralize every evil that we see. We need an enormous stiffening up of intellectual fibre, and a lot of scientific coldbloodedness. We need to see cleanly and unflinchingly, and establish some direct connection between 1, our vision; 2, our intellectual and emotional expression, and 3, our expression. The English are far better than we. Their trouble nowadays is rather the will than the vision. My social philosophy is working around to a paradoxical desire for Tolstoyan ends through Nietzschean means; socialism, dynamic social religion, through the ruthless application of scientific materialism.

— Reading No. 29 —

THE AMERICANIZATION OF THE WORLD*

W. T. Stead, a British journalist, published in 1901 a book with the above caption as his title; the subtitle was "or The Trend of the Twentieth Century." Stead belongs in the tradition of Pownall, Cobden, and others who urged rapprochement between the United States and Britain. He was conscious of America's economic impact abroad, but his book included material on other phases of United States influence in many lands.

✓ ✓ ✓

That the United States of America have now arrived at such a pitch of power and prosperity as to have a right to claim the leading place among the English-speaking nations cannot be disputed. . . . The Briton, instead of chafing against this inevitable supersession, should cheerfully acquiesce in the decree of Destiny, and stand in betimes with the conquering American. . . . Has the time not come when we should make a resolute effort to realize the unity of the English-speaking race? . . . Instead of counting Britain and the United States as two separate and rival States, let us pool the resources of the Empire and the Republic and regard them with all their

* W. T. Stead, *The Americanization of the World* (New York, 1901), pp. 4, 5-6, 12-13, 23, 164, 176, 181, 248, 266-267, 268, 269, 332, 333, 348, 350, 354-356, 356-357, 384, 388, 393, 396, 433, 440.

fleets, armies, and industrial resources as a political, or, if you like, an Imperial unit. . . . The question arises whether this gigantic aggregate can be pooled. . . . The question is prompted by the most solid of material considerations. Why should we not combine? We should be stronger as against outside attack, and what is of far greater importance, there would be much less danger of the fierce industrial rivalry that is to come leading to international strain and war. . . .

It is we who are going to be Americanized; the advance will have to be made on our side; it is idle to hope, and it is not at all to be desired, that the Americans will attempt to meet us half way by saddling themselves with institutions of which many of us are longing earnestly to get rid. . . .

[American economic strength and tariffs brought threats of retaliation, including those from Germany.] The watchword "America for the Americans" must be answered by the rallying cry "Europe for the Europeans," said the *Fremdenblatt*. . . . In Berlin the German Industrial Union have expressed through their Secretary, Dr. Wilhelm Vendlandt, their views upon the subject. He declared that the time had come for some Bismarck to rise up and assemble the nations of Europe and throttle the American peril. Europe, he argued, could perfectly well be independent of the American market. . . . "I believe," he declared, "in fighting America with the same weapons of exclusion which America herself has used so remorselessly and so successfully. We propose to work for an all European Union. The commercial interests of the hour are paramount, and a discriminatory alliance of all European Powers, including England, will be the inevitable result of the American invasion." The idea of a European solidarity of interest [*says Stead*] as against the United States is a vain dream. What difference does it make to the Austrian agriculturist whether his goods are undersold by the produce of Danish dairies or by the pork that is raised on the Western prairies? . . .

In discussing the influence which the Americans have exercised upon the world at large, reference must be made to the one great international question in which they have uniformly been a potent force in favor of the cause of progress and civilization. I refer to the question of international arbitration. The principle of settling disputes between Sovereign States by reference to a judicial or arbitral tribunal formed the very foundation of the American Constitution. . . .

[*American religious influence in Britain.*] To those who have been brought up in the sectarian seclusion of the Anglican cult, it is difficult to realize the extent to which American books, American preachers, American hymnody, mould the lives of the Free Churches of this country. . . . There rises vividly before my mind's eye the bookshelves of my father's study in the days when I was a small boy in a Congregational Manse on Tyne-side. In the post of honor, formidable and forbidding to me, at least, stood the stately volumes which contained the writings of Jonathan Edwards. . . . On another shelf stood the works of Channing, the Unitarian. . . . Teachers and preachers of New England [and Britain] stood side by side, and were held in equal honor as supplying the spiritual pabulum for a Nonconformist household. . . . The systematized revival, the deliberate organization of religious services for the express purpose of rousing the latent moral enthusiasm of mankind, is a distinctly American product of last century. Wesley and Whitefield may have sown its seed, but it grew up across the Atlantic. Revivalism flourished in the United States long before it was acclimatized on this side of the water. . . . Sankey's hymns still hold the first place in thousands of places of worship throughout the British Empire. They are sung much more constantly, and by a much greater number of people, than any other songs, with the one exception of the National Anthem. . . .

The habit of giving is one of the Americanisms which have not yet been successfully acclimatized in the Old World. The first American to make a distinct impact upon the English conscience by the force of his example was [Mr. George Peabody, whose initiative in supplying funds for rehousing the poor inspired others to do likewise.] But no one has preached the gospel of wealth so vigorously and has begun to practice it of late years so munificently as Mr. Andrew Carnegie. . . . We should be glad to see British-born millionaires attempt to imitate [him]. . . .

The ingenuity of American mechanism, and the skill of American engineers, have been employed for a generation past in reducting the bread-bill of the British working man. Incidentally this has brought in its wake agricultural depression among a minority of our people, but the immense majority have fed and grown fat upon American harvests and the beef and pork of American farms. . . .

The Americans have brought to us a host of ingenious inventions and admirably perfected machines. . . . [Mr. Fred Mackenzie, in *The Invaders,* summarized with amusing exaggeration British indebtedness to America]: "In the domestic life we have got to this: The average man rises in the morning from his New England sheets, he shaves with 'Williams' soap and a Yankee safety razor, pulls on his Boston boots over his socks from North Carolina, fastens his Connecticut braces, slips his Waltham or Waterbury watch in his pocket, and sits down to breakfast. There he congratulates his wife on the way her Illinois straight-front corset sets off her Massachusetts blouse, and he tackles his breakfast, where he eats bread made from prairie flour . . . tinned oysters from Baltimore, and a little Kansas City bacon, while his wife plays with a slice of Chicago ox-tongue. The children are given 'Quaker' oats. At the same time he reads his morning paper printed by American machines, on American paper, with American ink, and, possibly, edited by a smart journalist from New York City.

He rushes out, catches the electric tram . . . to Shepherd's Bush, where he gets in a Yankee elevator to take him on to the American-fitted electric railway to the City.

At his office, of course, everything is American. He sits on a Nebraskan swivel chair, before a Michigan roll-top desk, writes his letters on a Syracuse typewriter, signing them with a New York fountain pen, and drying them with a blotting-sheet from New England. The letter copies are put away in files manufactured in Grand Rapids.

At lunch-time he hastily swallows some cold roast beef that comes from the Mid-West cow, and flavors it with Pittsburg pickles, followed by a few Delaware tinned peaches, and then soothes his mind with a couple of Virginia cigarettes.

To follow his course all day would be wearisome. But when evening comes he seeks relaxation at the latest American musical comedy, drinks a cocktail or some

Californian wine, and finishes up with a couple of 'little liver pills' 'made in America.' . . ."

[*Stead on America's stimulus*]: Great Britain is beginning to be energized by the electric current of American ideas and American methods. . . . Here and there all over the country we can see British firms adopting American methods, and beating the Americans at their own game. . . .

[There are] three of the American secrets which are capable of export. The first is Education; the second is increased incentives to Production; and the third is Democracy. . . . Until our working people who have a vote determine to use it to compel Parliament to give every English workman's child as good an education and as fair a chance of making his way to a university career (if he is bright enough) as he would have if he emigrated to the United States, nothing will be done. . . . The second cause of American success, which we could appropriate if we pleased, is that of improved methods of production. We want more machinery, better machinery, and we must not stint its output. . . . The third cause of American success which we can also appropriate is that which comes from the frank adoption and consistent application of the principle of democracy. . . .

What is the conclusion of the whole matter? It may be stated in a sentence. There lies before the people of Great Britain a choice of two alternatives. If they decide to merge the existence of the British Empire in the United States of the English-speaking World, they may continue for all time to be an integral part of the greatest of all World-Powers, supreme on sea and unassailable on land, permanently delivered from all fear of hostile attack, and capable of wielding irresistible influence in all parts of this planet.

That is one alternative. The other is the acceptance of our supersession by the United States as the centre of gravity in the English-speaking world, the loss one by one of our great colonies, and our ultimate reduction to the status of an English-speaking Belgium. One or the other it must be. Which shall it be? Seldom has a more momentous choice been presented to the citizens of any country. . . .

[*Stead quotes A. W. Tourgée*]: "An alliance between

the great branches of the Anglo-Saxon family means the creation of a world-power against which it is not only impossible that any European combination should make headway, but it will have such control of the commercial and economic resources of the world as to enable them to put an end to war between the Continental Powers themselves without mustering an army or firing a gun. Whether they desire it or not, the necessities of the world's life, the preservation of their own political ideals, and the commercial and economic conditions which they confront, must soon compel a closer entente between these two great peoples. They are the peacemakers of the Twentieth Century, the protectors of the world's development, the protectors of free independence and of the weak nationalities of the earth." . . .

[*Quoting William E. Gladstone*]: What manner of man is the American of the future to be? How is the majestic figure, who is to become the largest and most powerful on the stage of the world's history, to make use of his power? Will it be instinct with moral life in proportion to its material strength? One thing is certain, his temptations will multiply with his power, his responsibilities with his opportunities. . . .

— Reading No. 30 —

"AMERICANISM" VS. "EUROPEANISM"*

Through the nineteenth century, and on into the twentieth, a kind of "war" went on between "Americans" and "Europeans." Not all the "Americans" lived in America,

* Henry James, *The Letters of William James* (The Atlantic Monthly Press, Boston, 1920), Vol. II, pp. 100, 101, 105, 304-305. Reprinted by permission.

nor all the "Europeans" in Europe. Expatriates from the New World found the Old more congenial, while the dissatisfied in Europe asked for more rapid Americanization. William James, the American philosopher, in the following extracts from his letters, gives expression to this conflict, along with his affection for Europe.

✓   ✓   ✓

[*To Wm. M. Salter Bad-Nauheim, Germany, Sept. 11, 1899.*]

We must thank God for America; and hold fast to every advantage of our position. Talk about our corruption! It is a mere fly-speck of superficiality compared with the rooted and permanent forces of corruption that exist in the European states. The only serious permanent force of corruption in America is party spirit. All the other forces are shifting like the clouds, and have no partnership with any permanently organized ideal. Millionaires and syndicates have their immediate cash to pay, but they have no intrenched prestige to work with, like the church sentiment, the army sentiment, the aristocracy and royalty sentiment, which here [in Europe] can be brought to bear in favor of every kind of individual and collective crime. . . . Damn it, America doesn't know the meaning of the word corruption compared with Europe! Corruption is so permanently organized here that it isn't thought of as such—it is so transient and shifting in America as to make an outcry whenever it appears.

[*To Mrs. Henry Whitman, Rye, England, October 5, 1899.*]

I am very glad indeed, too, to be in an English atmosphere again. Of course it will conspire better with my writing tasks, and after all it is more congruous with one's nature and one's inner ideals. Still, one loves America above all things, for her youth, her greenness, her plasticity, innocence, good intentions, friends, everything.

[*To Miss Pauline Goldmark, England, July 2, 1908.*]

And on the whole, what a magnificent land and race is this Britain! Everything about them is of better quality than the corresponding thing in the U.S.—with but few exceptions, I imagine. And the equilibrium is so well achieved, and the human tone so cheery, blithe and manly! and the manners so delightfully good. . . . Yet I believe (or suspect) that ours is eventually the bigger destiny, if we can only succeed in living up to it. . . . Meanwhile, as my brother Henry once wrote, thank God for a world that holds so rich an England, so rare an Italy. . . .

But profound as is my own moral respect and admiration, for a *vacation* give me the Continent! The civilization here is too heavy, too *stodgy*, if one could use so unamiable a word. The very stability and good-nature of all things (of course we are leaving out the slum-life!) rest on the basis of the national stupidity, or rather unintellectuality, on which as on a safe foundation of non-explosible material, the magnificent minds of the élite of the race can corruscate as they will, safely. . . .

— Reading No. 31 —

THE SECRET OF AMERICAN PROSPERITY *

The economic growth of the United States has fascinated its own citizens as well as observers from all over the world. In the following selections European visitors, from the end of the nineteenth century to our own time, give their impressions of workers in the United States. Selections toward the end of this group come from British productivity team reports, 1950. Teams of Europeans came to America to study productivity in our industry.

✔   ✔   ✔

Whether they liked what they saw or not, most foreign

* R. W. Smuts, *European Impressions of the American Worker* (Columbia University Press, New York, 1953), pp. 3, 4, 5, 6, 10, 11, 12, 15, 16, 17, 19, 21, 22, 23, 24, 27, 28, 34, 35, 38, 40, 44-45, 48, 56. Reprinted by permission.

observers did not doubt that America was a democratic society and that the circumstances of workers and the attitudes towards work and towards working people were very near the heart of American democracy. They did not mean, in any literal sense, that there was even approximate equality of wealth, social status, or power in the United States. They meant, first, that most jobs were almost equally respectable. Different occupations, of course, brought differences in prestige, but neither the occupation nor the prestige implied any fundamental difference in the value of individuals. . . .

The nonchalance with which Americans took jobs "beneath their station in life" astonished the Europeans. If a professional became a business official, Americans were not surprised. The son of a manufacturer was likely, as in Europe, to become an official in his father's business, but only in America did he expect to begin by working in the factory with his father's employees. The European university student who needed money might tutor or undertake some other form of intellectual work; but working one's way through college by tending furnaces or waiting on tables was (and still is) a unique American institution. More amazing to the European was the fact that the student could become a waiter or janitor temporarily without losing prestige. . . .

Many foreigners were dismayed by the "aristocracy of wealth" which they found in democratic America, and mistook it for a vulgarized version of the European aristocracy. More perceptive visitors, however, perceived a major difference. In Europe, being wealthy was an admirable condition, but getting wealth was somewhat disreputable. In America, working industriously at the acquisition of wealth was most respectable, but living idly on accumulated riches was reprehensible. . . .

While great fortunes and extreme poverty were obvious aspects of American life, foreign visitors saw also that relatively few Americans lived in want and that most lived in comfort and even luxury by European standards. . . .

Even the slums had a different appearance and significance for the European. H. G. Wells wrote: "To me, coming from London to New York, the effect of the crowd in the trolley-cars and subways and streets was one of exceptional prosperity. New York has . . . its . . . noise, disorder, discomfort, and . . . brutality, but to begin with one sees nothing of the underfed . . . dingily clad and grayly housed people who catch the eye in London. Even in . . . the filthy back streets of the East Side I found myself saying, as a thing remarkable, 'These people have money to spend.' In London one travels long distances for two cents, and great regiments of people walk; in New York the universal fare is five cents and everybody rides."

Many of the visitors, admitting that wages were far higher than anywhere in Europe, contended that the high cost of living in the United States restored the balance. As the visitors who investigated prices discovered, however, this was an error. The American worker did spend much more than the European, not because necessities cost more, but because he had the money and the inclination to spend it on comfort. . . .

Fresh from his amazement at the abundance of the worker's life, the visitor was astonished to learn that the worker was seldom content. Still, his dissatisfaction was not a matter of resentment or frustration; it was rather an impatient anticipation of better days to come. . . . The difference between America and the rest of the world was that all Americans were engaged in the same striving. Unlike their European counterparts, American workers did not believe that their effort was hopeless. . . .

A number of the English visitors admitted, with some astonishment, that here even the Irish were hard and efficient workers. According to a Hungarian nobleman and prelate: "There work is everything, and everything has become work. . . . One must keep moving; rest is not understood and is avoided whenever possible. . . . Labour represents . . . the potency of life; one might even say that the terms are . . . synonymous—that, in fact, work in the United States means life."

Even those who found the burden of work in the United States excessive admitted, however, that American workers did not seem especially conscious of working too hard. Harsh discipline was not particularly in evidence. . . .

Some of the keenest observers concluded that what appeared to be hard labor in America was not as demanding or fatiguing as it seemed. Appearances were deceiving. The American worked long hours (slightly longer than in England); he worked steadily, diligently, conscientiously; he produced more in the same length of time. Yet, he spent less physical energy than the European because he was provided with every facility to lighten and speed his task. "Hard work as it is understood in England only finds a hiding place in industrial America," observed an English trade-union official, and "as soon as it is discovered, a machine is patented which drives it out."

Combined with the mechanization of labor, observers found a degree of planning to eliminate unnecessary work and minimize work interruptions which was rare in Europe. . . .

American wage practice impressed the visitors strongly, as both an illustration and an explanation of the united effort of management and employees to produce more. The attention of the visitors was drawn not only to the uniformly higher level of American wages, but also to the entirely different outlook toward wages held by American employers. In Europe wages were a cost to be cut whenever possible; in the United States they were an incentive to higher production. "The evident desire of American employers," wrote an envious English trade-unionist, "is to increase wages, as the best means of encouraging efficiency."

Some of the visitors found that the attitude toward wages had its parallel in other facets of industrial relations. According to one English visitor, the European employer was concerned primarily with keeping the worker in his place, while the American was interested in getting the most out of him and had no compunctions about treating him like a self-respecting human being. The typical English businessman, as one of them admitted, . . . held himself aloof from his workers, and expected from them only subservience and obedience. The American, on the other hand, . . . was always approachable, and demanded initiative rather than subservience. The suggestion box was a peculiarly American phenomenon which delighted many foreigners.

The same concentration on production was reflected in factory conditions. In every respect which influenced output, conditions of work were admirable by European standards. In addition to the effort to expedite and ease work through machines and rational procedures, light, ventilation, space, and sanitation were generally far better than in Europe, especially in the newer factories. The fact that industrialization had come later to the United States was only partly responsible for superior working conditions. The English were astonished to find American factories comfortably heated in winter and sometimes even cooled in summer. . . .

The Europeans found the eagerness of employers to invest in machines highly unusual, but they were more surprised by the complacency of workers and unions in the face of new methods and new devices. One visitor reported that "labour-saving machinery is widely used everywhere and is encouraged by the unions and welcomed by the men, because experience has shown them that in reality machinery is their best friend." . . .

The difference between Europe and America with respect to the whole issue of productivity was neatly summarized by one of the English trade-union visitors. The British employer who wished to catch up with America, he advised, should "remodel and refit his factory on an up-to-date plan, get more in touch with his employés, provide them with a shop that has a degree of comfort about it, and give them a wage that will enable them to live at a somewhat higher standard . . . even if he asks them to do more work for the same." . . .

Industrial conflict in America was a man-to-man fight, with no quarter asked or given, unmitigated by the tradition of subordination on the one hand, or of benevolence and responsibility on the other. For all its bitterness, the strike in America was not a struggle against capitalism but against capitalists, not against the system, but for a bigger share of its benefits. And when the fight was over, the striker generally became an efficient worker again, whether he had won a bigger share or not. . . .

Class conflict in America, therefore, remained very largely a paradox to Europeans. They perceived that it was a struggle for the benefits of free-enterprise capitalism rather than an attempt to destroy it. But they failed to see that it was even more a struggle for power, with capital intent on preserving absolute control, and the unions on gaining for the worker a voice in the establishment of all the conditions of his work. The underlying issue was the traditional American right of each man to determine for himself the basic terms of his life. . . . Europe's most gifted Marxists . . . agreed . . . that there [was] no socialism among the American laboring class. . . . They agreed further that the basic reason for this was that the most highly developed capitalist economy provided the worker with a material prosperity and social respect unequaled in the world. . . .

Most of the [team] reports concluded that a major source of American efficiency is the "productivity-mindedness" of the entire industrial labor force. "Rather than machines," wrote the coal mining team, "we should like to see injected into the British industry the sense of adventurous urgency which characterises the American attitude . . . and is found in management and men alike." . . . "The Americans at all levels are much more receptive of new ideas than the British," wrote one of the teams, "and we felt that the introduction of new methods, equipment and machinery is welcomed more readily than it is in Britain." . . .

The basis of the American worker's attitude, the British agreed, is his intense aspiration for a higher material standard of living. . . . The American workman [said one team] is not a mere workman; he is an American and he aims to live as well as, and . . . to "have fun" to the same extent as any other American. . . . Having obtained his motor-car and his home . . . and clothed his family well, the American embarks upon the purchase of a refrigerator, television set, electric washing machine . . . luxuries to the British, but to the Americans essentials.

"It is generally agreed," according to one report, "that productivity itself is the goal and that, the more it is achieved, the greater the degree of 'full employment and "security" that will follow from it.' The British were astonished to find that in the coal industry, with its history of chronic overproduction and underemployment, the union actively encourages mechanization, "even in the certain knowledge that it will reduce the number of men employed; the union argues that wages will be increased and hours reduced for those that remain; more money will be available for improving working . . . conditions

. . . more and cheaper . . . [production] will create employment in other industries for the displaced." . . .

It was not the newness or the technical superiority of American machines which made the greatest impression, but the abundance of machines and power in relation to workers, and the widespread use of special purpose machines or fixtures, even for short production runs. The visitors declared that "wherever possible to save physical effort by using a mechanical aid, it will be done . . . contrary to British practice men were not expected to lift heavy weights, in fact, heavy lifting . . . was discouraged." . . .

The criticism of specialization on the ground that it destroys the satisfactions of work received little sympathy from the British. They were aware that, by contrast with the tasks of the British craftsman, the work of the American operative is frequently repetitive, . . . monotonous. . . . They concluded, nevertheless, that the advantages of the British system over the American are largely illusory. The variety of functions performed by the British craftsman in any one job is partially offset by the rigid barriers between jobs created by apprenticeship requirements and craft boundaries, both jealously guarded by the unions. . . .

In America, on the other hand, vertical and horizontal mobility are relatively easy, not only because of the shorter training required to learn a specialized job, but also because of the practical impossibility of maintaining rigid union barriers between quickly learned skills. "The field of operations of American workmen is . . . more flexible," stated one team. "An American employee may be assigned work outside his normal work. . . . Among British trade union members [such] resiliency . . . does not always find favour."

Some of the teams found that [in America there was] a radically different conception of the structure of society: "It is recognized that the man who can use his hands qualifies for the same amenities as the man with the brains. Both respect the other's capabilities. Both realise that one would be lost without the other. . . . The American workman is not a workman in the sense of the word used in Britain. . . . It was seldom indeed that away from a plant, even in industrial areas, one saw a man who could be recognized as a workman. . . . The boss does not drive away in his car whilst the employee looks on from the end of a long bus queue. . . ."

Acceptance of change, confidence in the benefits of the machine, anticipation of constantly higher living standards . . . [were the] beliefs of Americans at the close of the nineteenth century. [Since then] the ethos of American industrial society [has remained] unchanged.

— Reading No. 32 —

THE UNITED STATES OF EUROPE*

For centuries men have dreamed of a United States of Europe. The United States of America provided more substance to the dream. In the twentieth century, particularly since World War II, the reality has come closer. No longer do "realists" dismiss it as an ivory-tower phantasy; they discuss it seriously in legislative halls and in high governmental places. Much of the progress that has been achieved in the past few years has been owing to the energy and imagination of Jean Monnet.

↑   ↑   ↑

When I look to the future I feel considerable optimism. After six years, we have come a long way. The European Coal and Steel Community exists. A treaty on Euratom should be signed soon. A common market is in prospect. And Britain has shown her interest in associating with it. In such a vast enterprise as the uniting of Europe, there are bound to be troubles ahead. But greater troubles have already been overcome.

* Jean Monnet, "The 'Silent Revolution' in Europe," *The New York Times Magazine,* Feb. 3, 1957, p. 51. Reprinted by permission of the author.

It is certain that today European unity is increasingly recognized to be less a technical problem than one of political will and, on the whole, the political will is growing. Despite appearances, the Suez crisis, by underlining the limitations of the power of the European nations separately and the fact that they are all subject to similar pressures, is likely finally to increase that political will.

A strong and prosperous United States of Europe, delivered from fear, can powerfully contribute to the cohesion of the Free World and to our common power to insure peace and progress. But the unification of Europe is not simply an aim for ourselves. It is a method with wider applications in an age when fanatical nationalisms are being born at the very time that other societies—and far more mature ones—are finding nationalisms inadequate for their needs.

Europe's nations, faced with the prospect of decline like the city-states of ancient Greece because they are too small, are making one of the century's greatest experiments in government in their effort to break the restraints of the past. It may well be through this new kind of federalism—a federalism that rejects nationalist excess because it was precisely the disastrous results of such excess which made it necessary—that the twentieth century will make one of its greatest contributions to the civilization of succeeding generations.

SELECT BIBLIOGRAPHY

R. G. Albion, *Square-Riggers on Schedule: The New York Sailing Packets to England, France, and the Cotton Ports* (Princeton, 1938).

T. C. Blegen, *Norwegian Migration to America* (Northfield, Minn., 2 vols., 1931, 1940).

J. B. Botsford, *English Society in the Eighteenth Century as Influenced from Oversea* (New York, 1924).

D. F. Bowers, ed., *Foreign Influences in American Life* (Princeton, 1944).

J. B. Brebner, *North Atlantic Triangle: The Interplay of Canada, the United States and Great Britain* (New Haven, 1945).

G. Chinard, *Les Réfugiés Huguenots en Amérique, avec une introduction sur le mirage américain* (Paris, 1925).

D. M. Clark, *British Opinion and the American Revolution* (New Haven, 1930).

E. E. Doll, "American History as Interpreted by German Historians from 1770 to 1815," *Trans. Amer. Philos. Soc.,* N.S. XXXVIII, Philadelphia, 1949.

H. N. Fairchild, *The Noble Savage* (New York, 1928).

B. Faÿ, *The Revolutionary Spirit in France and America at the End of the Eighteenth Century* (New York, 1927).

L. Fraser, *English Opinion of the American Constitution and Government 1783-1798* (New York, 1915).

M. L. Hansen, *The Atlantic Migration 1607-1860* (Cambridge, Mass., 1941).

R. H. Heindel, *The American Impact on Great Britain 1898-1914* (Philadelphia, 1940).

R. W. Hidy, *The House of Baring in American Trade and Finance* (Cambridge, Mass., 1949).

H. M. Jones, *America and French Culture 1750-1848* (Chapel Hill, 1927).

A. Jorns, *The Quakers as Pioneers in Social Work* (New York, 1931).

H. Koht, *The American Spirit in Europe* (Philadelphia, 1949).

M. Kraus, *The Atlantic Civilization: Eighteenth Century Origins* (Ithaca, 1949).

D. Jordan and E. J. Pratt, *Europe and the American Civil War* (Boston, 1931).

G. D. Lillibridge, *Beacon of Freedom: The Impact of American Democracy upon Great Britain 1830-1870* (Philadelphia, 1954).

F. P. Miller and H. Hill, *Giant of the Western World: America and Europe in a North Atlantic Civilization* (New York, 1930).

R. F. Nichols, *Advance Agents of American Destiny* (Philadelphia, 1956).

H. A. Pochman, *German Culture in America: Philosophical and Literary Influences* (Madison, 1957).

E. P. Richardson, *The Way of Western Art 1776-1914* (Cambridge, Mass., 1939).

J. Rossi, *The Image of America in Mazzini's Writings* (Madison, 1954).

R. E. Spiller, *The American in England: During the First Half Century of Independence* (New York, 1926).

Count Otto zu Stolberg-Wernigerode, *Germany and the United States of America During the Era of Bismarck* (Philadelphia, 1937).

P. C. Weber, *America in Imaginative German Literature in the First Half of the 19th Century* (New York, 1926).

A. P. Whitaker, *The United States and the Independence of Latin America 1800-1830* (Baltimore, 1941).

C. Wittke, *Refugees of Revolution: The German Forty-Eighters in America* (Philadelphia, 1952).

I should like to express my thanks to The American Historical Association for its courtesy in allowing me to draw upon my *The Atlantic Civilization: Eighteenth-Century Origins,* published by Cornell University Press (Ithaca, 1949) on behalf of the American Historical Association.

INDEX

VAN NOSTRAND ANVIL BOOKS already published